CONFESSIONS
FROM THE CLOSET

Would You Like to Know the Other Side?

serendipity

BALBOA.PRESS

A DIVISION OF HAY HOUSE

Balboa Press books may be ordered through booksellers or by contacting:

Balboa Press
A Division of Hay House
1663 Liberty Drive
Bloomington, IN 47403
www.balboapress.com
844-682-1282

Because of the dynamic nature of the Internet, any web addresses or
links contained in this book may have changed since publication and
may no longer be valid. The views expressed in this work are solely those
of the author and do not necessarily reflect the views of the publisher,
and the publisher hereby disclaims any responsibility for them.

The author of this book does not dispense medical advice or prescribe the use
of any technique as a form of treatment for physical, emotional, or medical
problems without the advice of a physician, either directly or indirectly. The
intent of the author is only to offer information of a general nature to help
you in your quest for emotional and spiritual well-being. In the event you use
any of the information in this book for yourself, which is your constitutional
right, the author and the publisher assume no responsibility for your actions.

Any people depicted in stock imagery provided by Getty Images are
models, and such images are being used for illustrative purposes only.
Certain stock imagery © Getty Images.

Print information available on the last page.

ISBN: 979-8-7652-2688-9 (sc)
ISBN: 979-8-7652-2689-6 (hc)
ISBN: 979-8-7652-2690-2 (e)

Library of Congress Control Number: 2022905989

Balboa Press rev. date: 04/19/2022

Contents

Part 4: Confessions of School

Part 5: Confessions of a New Way

Introduction

Have you ever wondered what it's like to be different? Not so different that anyone would notice but different enough that you notice? Have you ever wished to be let in on how it feels to lead a secret life? That answer is the basis of this book.

I hid my psychic abilities in the closet. I know I'm not alone. So many of us have an awakening story to share. The time has come to clean out the closet, beginning with the psychic to the spirit, to the epiphanies of spirituality. It's the journey of a lifetime, because it takes a lifetime.

Confessions are never easy. When you have a secret, the ability to live your life fully is held back like a dam refusing to let the water continue its course. When the blockage is removed, the outburst of everything held back comes forward with such force that all you see is the force. The details of the stream are lost in the torrents of letting it all out.

If I were to start with the end of my story, the full force of my story, I too would find it hard to believe. If I were to tell you about my spirit friends who guide and guard me, and further tell you that each of them has a name, would I lose some credibility? If I could somehow find the courage to tell you about the school in the sky where my spirit friends taught me lessons that helped me through some very rough times in my life, would you read on? If I protect myself by writing under an assumed name, would you understand?

I can defend both sides of the debate. I grew up experiencing both the normal side of reality and the spiritual side. I grew as tired of the war between the two sides as I did of the war within myself. I know now that you can never win a war unless you first resolve the differences between the two sides. I won't try to convert or convince you of anything. I will only show you what it's like to be psychic.

People who don't understand the psychic are afraid of the force and unaware of the beauty of the stream that feeds the force.

That is the setting for the divide, the two sides separated by misunderstandings. You and I can now learn to come together. My hope is that if you learn what the gift has to offer, perhaps the psychic part of me will no longer fear being punished or persecuted. There will no longer be a need for the dam that holds me back. I want to show you the beauty of the stream that feeds the river of the spirit. I want to share the gift God gave me. I want to be free.

If I can reveal to you what it's like to be psychic, then perhaps you will see in yourself the psychic spirit, which is a part of everyone. Then we will all be free to start using our abilities to create a better world. But once again, the intensity of the force will overcome you unless I start at the beginning. So, I will begin with the little trickles of psychic events that have contributed to an understanding of the psychic world and the spirits that dwell there.

This isn't the story of an expert; it is the adventure of the experience. This is the story of a common girl growing up in an unusual world. This is a story about a little girl who struggled against her psychic abilities. She wanted nothing to do with all the dreams and visions that set her apart from everyone. Punishment and ridicule were the responses when the child spoke of the things she knew.

She couldn't stop being psychic, so the young child had to learn to hide her abilities. Her psychic experiences became skeletons in her closet no one should ever discover. This became the story of an adolescent who hid from her psychic abilities as much as she hid them from others. The psychic side of her was uncharted territory that frightened her.

This is the story of a woman who had to find the courage to accept what the child couldn't. She couldn't make the ability go away, so she had to learn to understand it. The woman opened the door to the closet and peeked into what was on the other side of reality.

This is the story of a mother who had nowhere else to turn when her daughter was hurt. This angry mother threw open the door on the other side of the closet and created a corridor to get access to the information needed to solve the crime the police had given up on.

This is the story of a wiser woman who learned not to seek punishment but to allow peace. The angry mother wanted to hurt the man who had hurt her daughter. The spirit taught healing instead. I never did get the vengeance I wanted, but I got what was needed.

This is the story of a woman who finds closure for many issues that started in lives gone by. I'm not done yet, so this is also the story about a beginning yet to be. I am getting ahead of myself here. The dam has broken, and the force is too much to handle. Let me start the story at the beginning, with the life of the little psychic who had so much to learn.

This isn't a story about the psychic realm. It is a story about having a closet and hiding in it. It is a story about anyone working with the spiritual realm. This is a story about the bridge between the two. The book has sections for you to respond and think, highlighted using italics. There is also room for you to take notes. You can keep track of your thoughts. Later, when you reread, you can see how much you have changed. In the beginning, the questions or statements are intended to seek support. As we grow together, the questions change to what you have experienced. Join me on the journey.

Many years have passed since I started this book, many years of not only learning but also living. When I was younger, I needed to learn about being psychic. As I got older, I needed to learn about spirit. Spirituality was enveloping me as the years went by. The next generation of being psychic is being spirit.

I desperately wanted to find a book or instructor so I could find guidance on this matter. There was nothing to be had, nothing in this world. My guides, my friends, were here to provide what I was looking for.

The years were full of training. It isn't enough to learn about being psychic. It isn't even enough to learn about spirit. You must live it. You must work on it. You must earn it.

This section is the stepping-on-toes one. I am now an older and wiser version of myself. Like all great plays, my life is a three-act play. My schooling taught me I had to give back. In the opening act you learn, then you live it, and then you teach it. Earlier, I lacked the courage to share some of the teachings. I had no idea how to finish the book, so I stopped writing.

Now, I know I must finish the book. Living with my friends, guides, and guards (Team Serendipity), I know I can write the ending now. Somehow the path has been made clear to me, and I can get started. Somehow? Such a small word and yet so big. I was partway out of the closet and living my life for many years. I lived that life with one guiding light. Family first. I still had my friends from school, and now as friends, they often came to my house. I no longer went to school. School came to me.

Somehow the decks were cleared, and I can write again. My family has grown smaller. My daughter was killed in a car accident. My husband and son were still family. After forty-two years of marriage, my husband passed from cancer. My son is still family. My son is now in his forties and has a full life. He no longer needs me as much. The decks are clear. I can now write. As before, I still had no idea how to end this book or even really a desire to.

Then I became ill. I knew I had to finish the book. So here I am.

PART 1

Welcome to My Closet

1

Life before the Closet

Life is great when you are a child. You are free to discover all you can do. I learned to get dressed. I learned I had a secret friend. I learned to play with my brothers and sisters. I learned I could see stories in my mind.

I don't really remember learning all these things. These skills are just the natural day-to-day things you do when you are growing up. All these things happened so naturally that there isn't a special day I can point to and say, "I remember the first time I got dressed." I can remember that I had a favorite dress with little purses printed on the fabric. I can remember because there was a special purse that matched the dress. I would put a few pennies in the purse and go to the store to buy some candy. This is a very vivid and special memory.

I can remember seeing things in my mind and excitedly telling people about them. I enjoyed the looks of surprise on their faces when they couldn't understand how I knew these things. This was a favorite game I loved to play.

I can remember playing in the yard with my brothers and sisters. There were six children in my family. I was the second from the youngest. We would have our friends join us and play capture the flag. Seeing twenty kids playing this game in a four-block radius was a joy to all. Even the grown-ups watched. Childhood was a joyous time.

I can remember my Old Man Friend. He always wore a brown robe that touched the tips of his sandals. He would come and teach me things he said I needed to know. He showed me ants and explained that they went about their business and lived in a separate world that functioned all by itself. He said my visions and hearing were like this. The ants were real, and so were the secret things I did.

There is a picture of me in my special dress. This verifies my memory. How can I prove my memory of my secret side? I asked an aunt of mine what she remembered of me as a child. She said I had been bright, lively, and always happy. My aunt said I'd had an odd habit of telling people things and then saying, "But you didn't know that did you?" Then I would laugh and be on my merry way. She said she didn't remember anything I spoke of. She assured me I was very charming.

These are my special memories of early childhood, when everything was new and exciting as well as safe and uninhibited. This was before I started to grow up.

Would you call my old man an imaginary friend? Would you call him a guide? The divide has started.

_____

_____

2

Learning about Closets

Life is great when you are learning how to do things. Life isn't as sweet when you are told you cannot do these things anymore.

I remember playing with my brothers and sisters. We put blankets around our back porch, crawled under it, and pretended it was a cave. I knew what pretend was.

I can remember telling my brother what I knew was going to happen. I always somehow knew when someone was coming over for a visit. When the visit happened, the look of surprise on my brother's face always made me laugh. I had apparently pulled off this trick one too many times because the look of surprise on his face was replaced by a look of fear.

I had learned by this time that not everyone had this inner knowing that lets you know things you have no obvious way of knowing. I hadn't yet learned why this talent made people upset. All I knew for sure was that I loved to tease my brother. I told him my secrets just to get a rise out of him. He ran to my mother, crying and yelling, "Make her stop. Make her stop." Suddenly, I wasn't a cute, little kid anymore. I was punished and told I shouldn't make things up anymore.

I was confused. I wasn't making it up. I knew what pretend was. I knew the difference between pretend and real. I also knew what a lie was. I could see a gray cloud pass over a person when he or she lied. I was punished just the same. I can still remember my brother sticking his tongue out and saying, "Ne ne, you think you know it all."

I felt sorry for myself at this point. I sat there in all my unhappiness and cried. My Old Man Friend, who was part of the problem, tried to help. He was a spirit. No one else could see or hear him the way I could. My family said I was making him up. He was my imaginary friend. How could I believe him? I had been taught very early on to discredit the spirit world.

My saving grace was that I wasn't alone. My maternal grandmother could do the same things I could. Grandmother knew what I was going through. The story of this psychic ability begins before I was born. The story begins with my grandmother. God bless her.

3

My grandmother could play with cards and tell stories from the cards. Neighbors went to her about their dreams because there was a rumor that she had a way with dreams. In a hushed voice, Grandmother talked about her dreams and visions. Grandmother was a lot like me. My mother wasn't.

Grandmother had to keep her special side secret. She had married into a family that was intolerant of any such nonsense. The strict Catholic family she had become a part of looked upon Grandmother's ways as silly superstitions.

Grandmother helped me to know that our shared secret was natural and good. She said very few people were as lucky as we were. Other people didn't see the goodness in what we could do. I was grateful to have a friend in my closet with me. Life was still good, even if I couldn't talk about certain things.

Would you also punish the little girl who just knew things? Would you be like my grandmother, who loved me anyway?

_____

_____

3

The Family Closet

One thing we can all agree on, whether we are psychic or not, is that we grow up with missing pieces. It's like a puzzle only partly put together. We have an incomplete picture of the way things are. We pretend to understand everything and play along, hoping to have a more complete picture later. If something doesn't fit where we think it should, we set the pieces aside. Unfortunately, sometimes the pieces get lost before we finish the puzzle. We never go back and fill in the holes. There are more pieces to my puzzle.

The setting of my life is an important factor in the way I lived. I was born toward the end of a family with six children. I was also born toward the end of my parents' marriage.

Mother divorced my father when I was only three. Mom was alone to raise six children by herself, so the rest of her family pitched in. My aunts and grandmother, therefore, had a great influence on me. I am grateful for the wide variety of examples that framed my life.

It was a different time when I grew up. It was a time when everybody's business was everybody's business. There was a strange mixture of truths and lies. Everyone knew why my mother had divorced my father, but no one would ever talk about it. I heard the aunts talk about "those poor children." I just never knew why. My inner knowing didn't extend into knowing it all. The reason for the divorce wasn't in the minds of my family members because they lied even to themselves about the problem. There was nothing on the subject in their minds to read.

Keeping my visions secret became easy, because no one ever asked too many questions. There were too many secrets in my family. Secrets were a way of life in my family; they were what I was taught. "If I don't admit that I am psychic, then I will be normal. If we don't admit that Dad is an alcoholic, then there isn't a problem. If we keep the incest a secret, then it never happened."

This is where my story begins. It began before I was born. This is how I learned about closets.

The young child I was learned well about secrets. Grandmother kept her secret about her abilities, and my mother kept her secrets about our father. I could live with my extra knowing hidden forever. Or so I thought. Secrets are like the water behind the dam. The pressure builds up until they simply must come out. My life illustrates the fact that secrets never die. They come back to haunt you.

Do you remember secrets you had to keep? Did you finally let them out as you grew older?

_____

_____

4

Closing the Closet Door

My psychic abilities and my family history played a part in my life, but they weren't an all-consuming factor. I was a normal child growing up in a wonderful era. It was the sixties, after all, a time of finding new freedoms.

Life was good. I started school with the naivety of a young child. School would teach me what I needed to know. I went to a private Catholic school, where fitting into a mold was very important. The problem was, I didn't fit.

I knew the experiences of the psychic world weren't to be talked about in public, so I kept my secret at school. School would teach me about the real world. I was an eager student. I wanted to learn everything.

The Catholic religion likes to teach about saints and sinners. Everyone wants to be a saint. Sinners were people who didn't do what the church said.

I loved the stories of saints. Joan of Arc heard voices just like I did. The children of Fatima saw things just like I did. The saint stories were full of psychic events just like my closet was. Maybe the psychic experiences I was having were real. They must be real. Why else would the school talk about such things?

I thought the nuns at school would understand my secret. They would help me. I was sure they would understand. I began to look at the nuns as my friends.

I had another one of my visions about this time. I saw a storm window fall from the second story of the building across the street. The window fell on a little boy and hurt him. I thought the nuns would help me stop this event from happening. I confided in a teacher and asked for her help. My teacher just laughed at me.

Two days later, when the window fell and hurt the little boy, I was in trouble. The nun called me a "devil child," and I was told to pray for salvation, or I would be cast into hell forever. Slam went the door on my closet. I vowed never to open it up again.

Would you call me names and tell me I was going to hell? Would you tell others to keep an eye on me because I was no good?

5

Unsafe in the Closet

I continued living a life torn between two worlds, my human side denying the truth I knew existed in my closet. I would have nothing to do with the psychic side, which kept getting me into trouble. I didn't want the reality of my closet intruding on my real life.

Grandmother and I rarely talked about the secret. Grandmother was a loving and kind woman, but I had also heard my aunts talk about her when she wasn't around. My grandmother, my mentor, was forgiven for her ways because she was only a convert to the Catholic faith. I had been born a Catholic. I knew I would never be forgiven for the terrible things I could do.

All my aunts thought they were better and wiser than Grandmother because they didn't believe in the psychic world. "A good Catholic never believes in such things," I was told. I was only seven years old and studying for confession and communion when my grandmother died. I wasn't prepared to be left alone with my secret.

My Old Man Friend was willing to help. He told me Grandmother wasn't really gone. I knew this was true because Grandmother still came to visit me. Our secret meetings were one more truth I could never share with anyone. This was one more thing to put in my closet.

The world was telling me my secret friend was an imaginary friend. The world told me Grandmother was gone. Then why did I keep seeing her? What was real, and what wasn't? I was doing my best to fit into the real world of my family and school. Real became what I could touch. Everything else had to go into my closet.

Let me now explain how I knew what would have to go in my closet and what wouldn't. When I see things, this isn't with my eyes. It is like a daydream. I am aware of when I am seeing the world and when I am seeing my visions. This is the same thing as knowing when you are seeing the world or watching television. I know what is real. I know what is pretend. I know what is psychic.

Will you come over to my side just a little when you understand how it happens?

6

Why I Hid in My Closet

I took refuge in my closet because I was safe in there. I was a child, and I was scared. I had heard what the real world did to people like me. If people suspected that I was psychic, they would make me an outcast and call me "evil" and "dangerous." This treatment was something I had already experienced firsthand.

If people knew I saw and heard things, I would be locked up and accused of being crazy. If people knew what I did, they would call me a "witch," and I had heard about what they did to the witches in Salem. Even the stories of saints gave me no comfort anymore. There is a dark side to these stories. St. Joan of Arc was burned to death. Many of the apostles were stoned to death. They were killed because they wouldn't deny their secret side. Even the most blessed of all was hanged on a cross to die. What kind of chance did I have if I came out of the closet?

I did what every child would do. I hid my ability. I pretended it wasn't there. I didn't want to get rid of my talents. Even at an early age, I realized how valuable they were.

I don't have a good data memory. I cannot spell or remember the multiplication tables. I could sit in class and just know the answers. School was always easy for me. I never studied and always got good grades. My third-grade teacher saw this spark in me. This teacher said I could be the first woman president if I could only learn to spell.

I hid in my closet because it was safe. I stayed in my closet because I liked it there. I am not the way I am because I fail to be like everyone else. I am the way I am because I like myself that way. I wouldn't trade places for anything.

Would you also love the secret abilities? Any ability will make your life easier. Would you want to keep them too? What ability do you keep to yourself?

_____

_____

7

The Other World in My Closet

"There is something in me that keeps me yearning, pushing me forward and teaching me learning." This is a quote I have heard echoing through my mind all my life. What is it inside each of us that makes us so different from everyone else? What is it inside each of us that makes us so much of what we are?

Throughout all time, the different religions speak of a soul, a seed, and a spirit. To find out about psychic events, we must learn more about where we came from. The young child I once was opened a door and let me look at myself more completely. I found out who and what I was.

I was ten years old when I found out what that something inside me was. I was back in my hospital room after having my tonsils removed. I coughed, and suddenly hot blood was choking me. I remember I had to keep swallowing it to keep from choking and drowning. I couldn't call out or get up because I was still groggy from the anesthesia.

A part of me got up and ran into the hall to look for help. I pointed to myself, still in bed, and pleaded for someone to help me.

Nobody would help me. Nobody could hear me. I did the logical thing for a child. I said to myself, "Well, nobody ever listens to kids anyway. I'm going to go play." I played as no child had ever played before. I walked all around the hospital; nobody could tell me to stop and behave myself. I enjoyed looking at all the rooms, machines, and people. Things were different now. I could go anywhere I wanted. I couldn't touch things, but I could look at them. I was enjoying myself.

A new friend walked with me. She was explaining things to me. She was the prettiest person I had ever seen. She said I was a good girl. "You aren't bad for the things you do, just different." She said it would be good to walk a different path. I should keep my secret things. She also said I should grow with the secret side as well as the solid side.

I suddenly found myself back in my body when I heard a doctor yelling, "Get a light down there, damn it. I can't see a thing." I remember thinking he was going to be in trouble for swearing.

The next few days were fun too. I was forbidden to talk because of the extra stitches in my throat. I noticed that I could hear everyone thinking. I wanted to tell all of them this, but I couldn't talk. I heard the nurse thinking about the little boy across the hall. The nurse felt sorry for him because he was an orphan and had no one with him.

I got out of bed and silently went across the hall to be with the little boy. I held his hand and stayed with him until they rolled him into the operating room. I heard the nurse wondering why I was doing this. I thought back to her that he was alone, so I had come to help. The shocked look on the nurse's face revealed she had heard me.

That look of fear let me know that everything that happened must be put in my closet. The mind reading evaporated after about a week. I kept the memory of my walking around the hospital.

I was so excited about this. I knew my Old Man Friend was a spirit. Now I knew I was a spirit too. I knew I could sometimes hear people thinking, and now I knew why I could do this. I found out that day that I was a spirit. This experience cleared up so many of my questions. I had opened the door to the other side.

Would you recognize this event as a near-death experience (NDE)? Do you think it was an out-of-body experience (OBE)? Would you just accept being different?

_____

_____

8

Immaterial in My Closet

All the things that couldn't be were kept in my closet. The problem I was facing was that the impossible kept happening to me. That is what it feels like when you are psychic. You don't make something happen; it happens anyway. A psychic event is like getting a telephone call. You cannot make it ring, but when something is there, you can pick it up. I don't want to answer the phone. I want to live my life like everyone else without all the extra knowing that initiates more questions. Questions I cannot answer.

This is the view you get when you shift your focus. We have all seen the two faces that look at each other and create a vase between them. That is what happens when you live between two worlds. You can see both images. Both are right next to each other.

The real world is supposed to be the world of matter and substance, but I have found that what really matters is in the world without substance. We all live in the material world, yet I find that the things of the world are immaterial. They have no real value. When you shift your focus, things change.

My Old Man Friend stepped into my world to guide and guard me. I had stepped into his world when I left my body behind in the hospital room. My psychic life is formed when the two worlds intersect and merge into each other. I shift my focus from being human to being spirit, and I see things differently.

The lines between my closet world and the real world aren't always clear cut. My Old Man Friend and my visions aren't real and can therefore easily be put in my closet. Where can I put the things that happen in the real world?

Life has a way of leading you where you don't want to go. The next story happened in the real world. I didn't want the psychic side of me to affect the real world. Some psychic events cannot be put in the closet because they are a part of the real world.

When my grandfather died, he didn't come to visit me as my grandmother did. I was touched by his death in another way. Grandpa was laid out in a funeral home near the house where we lived. The hours spent at the funeral home were interrupted only by the trips home to eat and sleep. It was during one of my trips home that Grandpa or something touched me.

The funeral home was within walking distance of our house, so my mother felt safe in sending me home for lunch. When I came to a certain corner, I suddenly became dizzy and couldn't walk or see. My brother's friend found me there, lying on the ground. He picked me up and took me home. Weeks later I found out that I had passed out at the very spot where Grandpa had been walking when he had his heart attack and died.

I don't know whether this story belongs in the closet. It happened in the real world. The two worlds do intersect at times. All I know for sure is that I never walked past that spot again. I could handle my closet when it wasn't real. I didn't know what to do when it became real.

Would or could you start to see how the other side affects you? Would you wonder about it as much as I did? Do you secretly wish you could too?

_____

_____

9

Normal in My Closet

I have no idea what normal is. I do know what is normal for me. My saving grace is that I'm not a very good psychic. My psychic impressions intrude into my life on an irregular basis.

I was free to live a normal life because I was normal.

In high school I was president of my sophomore class. I played basketball and even made captain of the team one year. I tried out for cheerleader and didn't make the team. I went steady with the boy down the block for three years. I was normal.

I discovered that if I ignored my psychic impressions, they didn't happen as often. I had no room in my life for this psychic stuff. I was busy being a teenager. I had time for nothing else except fashion and friends. I was normal.

I could still get good grades in school—not because I knew all the answers but because I knew what the teacher wanted to hear. I wasn't normal. I wanted to be normal. I didn't want to believe in all the unbelievable things that kept happening to me. I didn't have the luxury of denying the secret side of myself like normal people do. I wasn't normal.

The truth of the matter is, I enjoyed being psychic. It was the only way I knew to live my life, and I was comfortable with it. Being psychic played only a minor role in my life. My psychic abilities contributed lots of little things that could easily be put into my closet—for example, like the time a coworker came to bring me flowers in the hospital after I had my appendix removed. He stood there in his bib overalls and talked about how he had picked this plant because it had "all these ball things that turn into flowers."

My secret side told me not to laugh at this man because he would become my husband. My normal side protested and said, "Oh no! This man doesn't even know those ball things are called 'buds.'"

My years of experience had taught me one important thing about the inner voice. It always knew what it was talking about. We were married within a year. I felt an obligation to warn my fiancé that I could do a few odd things.

The man made no claim about being psychic and didn't even believe in being psychic. He admitted, however, that he remembered a dream where he saw me on a buckboard. In the dream, he had felt a need to save me. The only other thing he remembered about the dream was that I had purple lips.

My poor husband didn't have a clue about what he was getting into. To be totally honest, I didn't know either. If I had known, I would have aborted my mission. I was about to lose my comfort zone.

We were married only a year when the reality of my closet imposed itself once again on my life. This time it was a biggie. This time it was something I couldn't ignore. This time not only was my life threatened but also the way I lived my life was taken from me. My psychic side wouldn't be silenced.

The doctors had found a tumor in my large intestine. In retrospect, all I can say is that I understand why it was there. The tumor was near the chakra where my feelings were kept. I had spent the first twenty-four years of my life hiding my feelings. You learn to hide your feelings in an alcoholic setting. It wasn't a healthy way to live my life. My feelings were stuck, and my secret side had to find a way to let me let them out.

Would you trust your extra talents? Would you hide from them as much as you hide the things you do? Do you question why this had to happen?

_____

_____

10

The End of My Closet

The lines between the real world and the psychic one aren't clear cut for me. I'm not sure if it was a near-death experience or just another one of my journeys. The landscape of my adventure away from my body resembled a near-death experience. Whatever it was ... it would change me forever.

The details of this experience aren't what I wish to share with you. Many people have already explained the journey through their personal accounts of a near-death experience (NDE). My wish is to share with you what it feels like. I hope I can reveal enough of the experience so you can also feel it in your soul.

When your spirit first exits the body, the feeling you get is of complete acceptance. Is it any wonder that water is the symbol of spirituality? When you dive into water, it surrounds and accepts you just the way you are. You are greeted and made to feel welcome. The feeling of acceptance overwhelms you, and you wonder what could possibly be better.

As you grow into the experience, the experience grows into you. You review all that has happened in your life. The feeling of understanding overcomes you, and you wonder what could possibly be better.

You slowly adjust to your surroundings. You realize that acceptance and understanding are changing into something more. The feeling of water grows thicker and warmer around you. The feeling of such immense and total love embraces you so you wonder what could possibly be better.

You wish to stay right where you are forever, but the experience continues. You realize you are traveling. It is the same feeling you get if you close your eyes in a moving car. You know you are going somewhere, but you are making no effort to move. You are caught up in a current.

The realization that you are headed somewhere leads you to question why the surroundings seem to be growing brighter. It's like when you sit outside on a summer day. You realize the warmth is coming from the light. You suddenly know you are heading toward the light.

At some point in your travels, you realize that whatever is separating you from your surroundings is beginning to dissolve. You become one with "all." I cannot begin to tell you what this feels like.

There is nothing else to which you can compare it. I can tell you there is a reason why all the great religions speak of a "one," a "one God," and an "all." They speak of it because it is true. The religions tell us we are a part of this "all." This is the feeling you get when you travel this far. Suddenly there is nothing that separates you from "it."

Although I don't quite remember the details, I will never forget what happened next. I knew everything. Everything I ever wondered about, I knew. Every injustice I ever fought against, I understood. Every question I ever had, I answered. Everything made sense.

Everything was wonderful just the way it was because everything had a reason. Everything fit together perfectly. In this knowing of everything, I knew I had to go back. I didn't want to go back, but even going back to life brought me no pain because I knew that ...

Suddenly I was me once again. Once you have been a part of the "all," the "all" never leaves you. My life is different; I am different. Life goes on.

Do you recognize this event as another NDE? Do you want to be changed forever?

11

Cleaning the Closet

Big changes were made in my life as a result of this unwanted out-of-body experience at the hospital. My psychic abilities tripled. I couldn't fit one more thing into my closet. I had no other choice. I had to clean out my closet.

Cleaning a closet isn't a pleasant job. It is put off as long as possible. I wasn't looking forward to looking at all the things I had accumulated over the years. I didn't want to face who and what I was. I was afraid of myself.

Self-preservation forced me to look at my closet and myself. Because I wasn't all there anymore (half my large intestine had been removed along with the tumor), I had no place to keep my feeling anymore. Whenever I tried to keep things inside myself, I got flu-like symptoms.

I am normal. I am very human and very stubborn. It took three years for me to build up the courage to look at my closet. For three years I fought with myself about facing what was in my closet. It took three years of pain to realize I had to change the way I was living my life. I was more stupid than stubborn because I was running from the very thing that would save my life. I was running from my spirit.

I was very sick during this period of my life. I was often sent to bed because all the color in my face was gone. I was weak and tired. I was living with flu-like symptoms for three years, and it was draining my strength. I was fading away because there was nothing left inside me. My secret self was banished because I was afraid of where I had gone when I died. I wasn't yet ready to work with my spirit side. I didn't yet realize that I would need my spirit side if I wanted to live.

My body was in revolt. My inner side was demanding to be known, and my outer self would have nothing to do with it. My inner fear wouldn't allow myself to face my psychic side. My body could no longer handle the emotional battle within. As in any war, the battle zone is ugly. The battle zone in my body wasn't allowing my surgery sight to heal. This was showdown time with my spirit, and my spirit was winning.

My greatest fault, my saving grace, is my temper, my feelings. My health didn't get better until I got really mad. *Mad* is the appropriate word to use here. Out-of-control emotions express the feeling of being mad but not having madness. I awakened the part of me that was asleep. The dam had broken. I felt sorry for the poor doctor who stood in the way.

I was undergoing another medical test to see whether any of the tumor was left in me. I was still bleeding internally and was in a lot of pain. I had explained to the doctor that ever since the surgery, I'd had adverse reactions to many medications and didn't think I should be put completely under. He said not to worry and that I would be awake within an hour. He was wrong.

I awakened the next day with the doctor standing over me and apologizing to me for not believing how bad my intestines were. He had been under the impression that I was exaggerating my pain. My intestines looked like I was eating myself up inside. They were raw and bleeding, and there was fear that they would rupture.

I let this poor man experience my rage. "Why did you not listen to me? Why did you not believe me?" I'm still sorry for the injury I inflicted on him when I yelled at him. I knew what was eating me. I knew I had to clean my closet and learn to understand it. I had no other choice.

Have you ever fought with yourself? Did you finally change because it was best for you?

_____

_____

12

Let's Make a Deal

The only way I could deal with my closet was to make a deal with myself. I wouldn't keep putting things into my closet. I would deal with each new psychic adventure as it came my way. But I would not, I could not, I dared not get too involved with the psychic side of me. I would keep an open mind about what I was experiencing. I had no choice. I couldn't make it go away, so I had to find a way to live with it. I would meet myself halfway.

Have you ever gotten a wake-up call that forced you to change? If you experienced another one, would you hold yourself back as I did for many years? Would you be grateful that you changed, grew, and learned? What needs to change in you?

_____

_____

PART 2

Confessions from a Psychic

13

Psychic 101

There is a need to review what I already knew about being psychic from a human's viewpoint. Waiting in my future were more events that would erase the human vantage point. I had lived basic training in the field of being psychic because I was about to enter a period where I would need every psychic skill I possessed to continue in life. But for now, let's not get ahead of ourselves in this adventure. Let's start at the beginning with Psychic 101.

There is a story often told that changes with each telling. The further from the source it goes, the less it is revealing.

I have heard so much about being psychic. Not all of it applies to me. Perhaps it is like the telephone game we played as children. We would sit in a circle and tell a story into the ear of the person next to us. The story would continue around the circle until it was told once again to the original person. The original person would recognize parts of the story. Other parts had changed greatly.

There is a truth to the original experience. The story may get confused when it passes through many people. I was the first person on the phone line. My life was ground zero. Before I could step into the other side, I first had to face what I already knew.

Will you listen on as I come to terms with the other side? Will you call me names, or will you support me? Do you also need to face the spirit in you?

_____

_____

14

Explaining Life after Dying

I cannot verify to you what happened to me during my short stay in heaven. I can only show you how the experience changed me. There is life after death in the spirit world, and there is life after death when you are made to return to the physical world.

After I returned from the wake-up call of being revived, more than my outlook was changed. I now seem to be operating through different channels. My central nervous system operates at a higher voltage. My mind races in a higher gear. My thoughts are an octave higher.

My journey to heaven didn't solve all my problems. In fact, it created more of them. I could no longer pretend I was normal. My experiences up to this point were like basic training. Being psychic is only a small part of being spirit.

Externally I didn't change. Inside me things were very different. My near-death experience affected my physical body as well as my attitude. There is a physical residue that affects you after you die. I have always been accused of being too sensitive. My body was now developing new sensitivities. I was getting further and further away from being normal.

Medicines react differently in me. Ibuprofen makes me high. Penicillin starts a painful reaction in me. Sulfa drugs do strange things to me. The metal of zippers and the rivets on my jeans create a rash. I am physically and emotionally too sensitive.

My body is unable to tolerate something as subtle as paint fumes. I have a hard time dealing with people in a bad mood because I feel something pushing on me when they get too close. I can feel anger, and physically it hurts me. I was so sensitive at one point that I could even catch a sunburn from people.

This is the only way I can express what it feels like inside. I had become a person sensitive enough to be able to pick up the subtle energies others cannot see, hear, or feel. I was now psychic.

Will you listen more, my friend, as I release the spirit inside me? Will you continue as I explain myself? Will you open to the spirit in you?

15

Explaining My Side

Despite the one difference of being psychic, I am abnormally normal. There is nothing about me that stands out except that I seem to be infused with a little more energy than the standard population. To others I appear a little scatterbrained, but that is because the scope of my thinking extends further than most people can see.

My early years taught me to hide the way I was different. When I came out of the closet, I realized I had wasted a lot of years living in the land of denial. I pretended to be like everyone else. I consciously slowed down when others were watching me. I realized I irritated the rest of the world with my exuberance. The flip side of this is that the rest of the world had the same effect on me.

I call the rest of the world the "mass majority" (MM). They are the part of reality that is "material minded" (MM). Einstein called them "mediocre minds" (MM), which have violent opposition to spirit. Collectively they are the MM.

I couldn't understand how people could be so slow. To show the MM what it is like, we can compare it to old record players. The MMs see me as a record being played at the high speed. They can't get it all, and everything is sped up. I see the MM as being played at the low-end speed. The MM appears to be slowed down and drawn out. I find this speed very hard to deal with. The MM wants to give people like me Ritalin to slow us down. I would like to give them speed to help them catch up. The bottom line is that records and people are made differently. When we let them play at the speed they were made for, there is beautiful music.

I had to live in the real world with the MM. I had to pretend to be like them. When I spoke of something I knew via my inner knowing, some people questioned how I knew that. I would lie and say I had read the information someplace. In high school one of my best friends resented my getting good grades in math when she knew I didn't know the multiplication tables. When I was in college, my computer teacher wrote a program that compared grades to how often we missed a class. I had the bad habit of skipping classes, but I always maintained good grades. He never did understand why I didn't fit into his theory. It was because I am what I am.

I couldn't understand how the MM couldn't see what I saw. The reality of the situation is that we were looking at the same thing from different views. I couldn't see the trees because I was looking at the forest. The MM see the trees, because they look for the physical reality. Both realities are real. My task is to learn how to integrate them.

I knew I was different but not so different that I couldn't relate to the MM. I am a very human spirit. I reside on both sides of reality. I am not the way I am because I fail to be like you. I am the way I am because I need to be that way.

The human side of the MM and me are like a simple sentence. Just the facts are enough for them. "The man ran the race." This pretty much says it all. The inner psychic side and the spirit want more. "The quick, lean man merged with the wind, which pushed him to the prize." This statement adds so much more to life. The MM are the nouns and verbs of our world. On the other side of us are the more expressive parts of speech, which improve upon the basic parts of speech. The MM are the tangible things in life. The psychic side of us allows us to enjoy the intangible things of life. I don't want a tangible world without intangible joys. I don't want a life. I want a good life.

The MM and the psychic (spiritual) world merge into each other in my life. I had to learn to address both sides of myself if I ever wanted to be whole.

Do you also know about the side that makes life better? Are you already awakened to spirit but don't know it? Do you want to start? I can show you how.

_____

_____

16

Explaining Your Side

I can see both sides of reality. I am human too. I understand and identify with the refusal to accept the semi-real world of my spirit. I refused to accept it, and it was happening to me.

I too tried denial of my spirit side. The mounting evidence outweighed my denial. I also feared the unknown, but the wonderful things I received outweighed my fear. I also couldn't believe, but I didn't have the luxury of not believing.

I had to overcome many obstacles to learn to accept my spirit side. I had to overcome all the misunderstandings and misinformation on your side. The human side was lacking. The normal side wasn't enough. This meant I would have to give up on being normal.

Believing in the other side meant I would have to give up what I had been taught to believe was true all my life. I started to investigate what others believed to be true. I wouldn't get into a long discussion on what truth is. I knew only that my truth included more than I had been taught. I had to stop believing and start working only from what I knew. I knew my spirit was real.

I couldn't give up believing what I knew to be true of the spirit side just because the normal world didn't experience what I did. It was much easier to give up on what the world thought was true. The real-world claims that visions aren't possible. Well, maybe for the real world they aren't possible, but for me they are. I will give you another example to show you what I mean.

I was sitting alone in my living room, reading the newspaper, when before my eyes was another vision. I saw people standing around and looking at something on the ground. There was great concern among the crowd. I saw a woman kneeling next to the unknown object and looking up imploringly at the gathering people. I heard the phrase "I don't know what to do." The woman looked back at the ground and knew she had to stop the pain before her. "What should I do?" she screamed.

"I don't know what to do" was the answer from the crowd.

That was the end of the pictures in my mind. I had been through this kind of experience before. I knew what I saw had already happened in the future. I knew there was nothing I could do but wait for it to happen.

It took two weeks for reality to catch up to my vision. I spent this time telling people about the scene because I needed to prove to the world and myself that the spirit was real. It was late at night when the screaming started. My family was asleep. Suddenly, cries of pain rang out in my daughter's room. I ran to her to see what was happening.

My eight-month-old, seventy-pound puppy had just discovered that my twenty-pound spaniel dog had gone into heat. The poor female was crying in pain as her little paws dangled there, six inches in the air. I knelt next to them and tried in vain to separate them. By this time the crowd had gathered. The rest of my family was awake. I looked up at my husband and said they were stuck. I asked my husband to help. He said, "I don't know what to do."

My daughter was screaming, "What's happening?" Sex education is a very important thing, and at this point, I wished that I had better prepared her for this.

I once again yelled at my husband, "What do I do?"

He laughed and said, "Well, I don't know what to do."

This time I had proved myself. I had told people about what was going to happen before it happened. This time I had proof. This time even I had to believe.

I won't argue the fact that many people don't experience psychic events. I can longer deny the fact that I do. There is another dimension for me. There is another dimension for you. We aren't one-dimensional people. We have another side. We have a spirit side.

We are multidimensional. I was just beginning to glimpse what this meant.

Do you know there is more to what is known? Do you also want to find out about this?

_____

_____

17

Explaining the Psychic

Everyone has the capacity to be psychic. The word *psychic* means having to do with the mind. We all have minds. We are all psychic. I'm not bragging or making unusual claims when I say I am psychic. Being psychic is like being able to sing. We can all do it. Some of us are just better at it than others.

Being psychic is on a sliding scale. The debunkers experience such a mild form of it that they cannot believe it is true. Many people experience it once or twice in their lives and can comfortably explain it away. Other people (me included) experience it to such a degree that it cannot be ignored. On the high end of the scale are wonderfully talented people who can work with it daily. The point I would like to make is that in whatever measure it exists, it does exist.

Being psychic is natural. Being psychic has causes and effects. The way I've come to understand being psychic is comparing it to the weather. I don't control it, and it doesn't control me. I have learned to read the signs. I know what the day will be like. I then dress appropriately.

Being psychic has its dry spells and its downpours. Other events in this biosphere interact together to create patterns and conditions. Science can now understand but not control or predict the weather. We have learned only to go with the flow. Science will one day understand the ability better and realize it has patterns and variations.

The psychic talent isn't good or bad. It is what we do with it that makes it good or bad. The gift is an awesome force, very much like fire. Poorly used or directed, it can be very destructive. Properly harnessed and utilized, these natural forces can and do transform the world.

The ability isn't a thing. It is a force. It is energy. You cannot point to it and say, "There it is." We can compare it to another force and from it get a clue on how to control it.

I have found that being psychic is like electricity. You will know it when you feel it. I believe there are receptors in our bodies that pick-up stimuli from the environment. I know this is true because I feel it.

Electricity is defined as an agent that produces various physical phenomena. It isn't a real thing. It is an agent, a force. A whole new science was introduced when we began to work with electricity. We invented new words like *amps* and *volts*. We learned about conductors and nonconductors. We had to learn to think in a whole new way to understand electricity. When electricity became common, it transformed the way we live our lives.

This is the challenge for science. A psychic phenomenon, like electricity, is an agent that produces various physical phenomena. It isn't a thing; it is an agent, a force. When the psychic force of our minds is understood and utilized, the transformation of the world will be phenomenal.

Are you still with me? Have you started wondering about it now?

18

Explaining Computers

There is one more way I can show you what it's like to be psychic. We can compare our minds to computers. Science has always said we are just processors of information. I believe being psychic is the new generation of computers.

Being psychic is like having windows in your computer. I can suspend a program, look something up in a master program, and then return to the original program. I love this example because ten years ago, this knowledge didn't exist. Computers have evolved and grown more complicated. We can do more and more things with computers as we come to understand more about them.

The ability is the mind's computer. We can hook up to other computers with our minds. We can get information from some far-off place. We can imagine and plan things in our computer minds. Yes, our minds are like computers, just like all the debunkers have always said. But look at all the things a computer can do. Imagine all the things that can be done in the future.

There is a whole group of people who choose not to understand computers. They don't wish to learn or work with computers. It is the same with our psychic abilities. We must learn how our psychic abilities work if we are to use them to their full potential.

Computers are a good way to illustrate how evolution is stepped up to a phenomenal pace. A few people worked on Windows 95 and then downloaded it to the rest of the population at large. Windows 98 and Windows 2000 quickly followed. We are now benefiting from the work of a few dedicated people.

I submit to you that there are those of us who are working on the equivalent of Spirit 2020. The new software of spirituality is the foundation of the New Age. Not everyone needs to participate in the evolution. The new way of life will come anyway.

Now I know you are with me. It isn't a matter of getting on board and joining. "It," spirituality, is all around now.

19

Explaining Coincidences

The debunkers love to claim that psychic events are just coincidences. A coincidence is when we cannot see the cause of what we are experiencing.

Case story: I had an urge to go into my daughter's school. I knew I had to go in. I didn't know why. Finally, I couldn't ignore the urge anymore. I made up a pretense of needing to talk to one of the teachers.

The two of us were standing by the office door talking. Unbeknownst to me, my daughter was in gym class and had just had an accident that broke her finger. She was on her way to the office to call me when she saw me standing there.

Is this just another coincidence? I don't think it is. This is just another example of the perfect timing between the material and psychic worlds. Coincidence is the psychic side of us peeking out and letting us know it is there. We are all psychic, whether we know it or not. Common occurrences such as this exhibit the ability. Understanding the cause of the silent knowing will require an understanding of the new science of mind. The definition of *psychic* is "of the mind."

A common analogy to understand how psychic perception works is to envision your life as a road. When your mind is operating from only the material side, it's like you are earthbound and cannot see very far ahead. When you begin to listen to your inner inspirational side, it's like you have an aerial view. You can now see what is further ahead of you. When you remove yourself from the material world, you can also see all around yourself. You can look behind and see whether you made a wrong turn. You can plan your route better because you can see the longer road. You can see all the intersecting roads and connections we call "coincidences."

It is a coincidence that my physical body illustrates how my psychic side leaks out. I am right-handed. I am left-handed. I am ambidextrous. I favor my right hand because right-handed people have it easier in this world. I can use my left hand as well as my right. I am a closet lefty. The added dexterity of my left hand helps me out as I go about my life.

The parallels between my hands and the material and psychic sides are obvious. This physical fluke is also the groundwork for the reason I am what I am. We are all aware that the brain has two sides. The hand that dominates implies which part of the brain is dominant. The dominant side of the brain indicates whether you are grounded in the hard-core realities of the world or free to create and explore the other side of our world. The coincidence is that I don't have a dominant hand or side of the brain. I am a combination of both.

The two sides of our brain work so well together that we forget they act very differently. Our psychic and physical sides also silently work together so well that they appear to be one. Most of the world hasn't yet learned to use both of their hands equally well. We tend to ignore our left hand and our psychic sides. The psychic ability is there, but we don't use it as much as we could. We need to practice using both sides of ourselves. One side should never dominate the other. I am a little of each. This puts me in a position to understand both sides of the conflict between the physical world and the psychic world. I'm logical enough to have earned a degree in computer programming, a very left-brained science. I am creative enough to enjoy writing as a hobby. This is a very right-brained talent. The question is, which came first? Did my brain make me able to understand both the physical and psychic worlds, or did my spirit influence the way my brain developed? Which came first, the chicken or the egg?

This is what I am experiencing. The deafening whisper of the inner self is what I hear. Most normal people choose to ignore and dismiss their intuitive selves. My inner self is just as stubborn as my outer self. It won't go away. It demands to be heard. It isn't a split way of seeing things; it is a dual way of seeing things.

From this position, I see things differently. What appears to be the magic or mystery of psychic events can be easily understood. From the perch of my higher view, I can envision a time when the mystery and the magic are understood. From my view, I can already see the connections.

To understand the other side of our mind, it will become necessary to step into our inner selves, the part we cannot touch. The part we can only feel. The part the debunkers dismiss and throw away. This part of us is the psyche, the soul, the spirit.

Are you taking a side here? Has the division started already? Can you welcome the other side and start to get it together? I can feel your anxiousness.

20

Explaining Destiny

Coincidence is one thread showing that there is a connection between you and others. Destiny is when many threads come together to create an outline of your life.

Destiny isn't my full-time job. Most of my life is spent simply being human. However, certain parts of my life are preplanned and "got to be." I also know in my soul that I must honor the decisions I made before I came to this body. This is how I define destiny: a promise to myself that I succeed at being me. My soul and I are in this together.

Destiny is the spirit in you crying out to be noticed. It is my destiny to openly admit I am psychic. There is a seed in my soul that needs to grow. I remember a time during a life gone bye when I was killed for being what I am. With my dying breaths, I knew that if others understood what it was really like to be psychic, then they wouldn't fear me.

I chose to incarnate into this life because I knew that finally I could be what I am and not be killed for expressing my psychic side. I write this book to give voice to the psychic side of me. My soul needs to reveal what it is and ask for understanding so the fear of being found out can be removed from me. I also write so the fear of learning more about yourself can be removed from you.

I am what I am, but I'm not all I am. I wish to explore the other side of me. I also need to know I won't be killed or condemned for doing so. I fear the human side more than I do the spirit. I fear for the human side even more because the spirit side is meant to compliment and assist the human side. Without the spirit, we are empty; we are without purpose. We aren't meant to compete. We are meant to complement.

Spirit and physical are the ultimate examples of yin and yang. The whole truth is that we aren't yin or yang. We are the yin *and* yang. We are both. One side serves and complements the other. We are the whole, not the part.

My life, my mission, is to be both human and spirit. I'm not a spirit having a human experience; nor am I a human who has a soul. I am both. It was only after being both that I realized I was now whole, complete. If you don't take sides, you are complete. I am.

Do you begin to wonder now about being one? Are you now reaching out to the other side? No division.

21

Explaining the Other Side

There are two sides to every story. There are even two sides to my closet. I can open a door on the other side and step into the land of make-believe. So much has happened to me that the other side has made me believe the unbelievable. I have seen enough of it to know.

The other side is limitless. It cannot be described because it extends forever. I can show you the sections I have been able to touch. I remember going beyond what is supposed to be on earth when I died as a child and played in the hospital. I also remember what it was like to go beyond what is supposed to be when I died as an adult and went to the other side. And the greatest part of the other side is meeting what is known as God.

This is the piece of information I keep hidden deepest in my closet, the part of me I was terrified to examine. My upbringing taught me where my place was in this world. I was a child of God. But just like with my earthly parents, I wasn't allowed to question or have an opinion. I never felt I could carve a relationship with God. The priests and nuns could but never me; I wasn't as good as they. Especially never me because I had this bad thing in me the nuns said came from the devil. That is why I was so surprised when I met him or her. He wasn't at all like what I was told. The rules of the game of life weren't at all like the religions make it out to be. When information is passed through too many hands, things get lost along the way. The original meaning is lost when it gets translated.

At this point in my life, I had yet to acquire the knowledge to understand and therefore become comfortable with what I am. I had no idea exactly what I was. For now, I like the simple sentence "I am." A sentence that is limitless and full of promise.

I had often asked myself, "Why am I here?" My Old Man Friend always answered with the same answer the world answered: "We are here to learn." Not knowing what it is you are to learn is difficult until you have learned it. Catch-22—I got you, so tell me now what to do.

On the other side, I found another answer to "why we are here." We are here to learn to change. Change takes time. Time is available on earth. We are here to learn to grow. Facing a challenge and learning from it make a change in us that is measurable on the other side.

Before I tell you more about the other side, I must somehow reveal to you the awful events that drove me to depend on my closet. I didn't change or grow until it was forced on me. I wouldn't step out of my comfort zone until it became totally uncomfortable. Hitting rock bottom hurts. It had to be. I planned all this before I was born to see whether I could change.

Will you give me the strength to handle things dear God? People say God won't give you things you cannot handle. At this point, I think God thinks too much of me. Will you give me strength?

PART 3

Confessions from an Adult

22

Overlapping Sides

My world, my reality, would never be the same again. The method of coping that had sustained me in the first half of my life was no longer available to me. I could no longer keep my secret side secret because my body rebelled whenever I tried. Keeping things inside after half my colon was removed now cost me the unpleasant side effect of being ill. Hiding from my secret side and myself was no longer an option.

Now whenever the psychic side peeked out, I examined the experience and paid attention to it. Later, I was able to learn from what was happening, but for now, it was all I could do to become a silent observer. I first had to learn to trust and understand these interruptions in my life. The two sides were overlapping and coming together.

One of the first psychic events that confronted me was seeing my son. There's nothing unusual about this except I was only two months pregnant at the time. I was lying in bed, watching television, and off to the side of the room, I saw a spirit. It was the spirit of a tall man-child. I sensed him there, neither standing nor floating, just watching me. His thoughts were focused on deciding whether he would choose to become the child in me.

I addressed him with my thoughts the same way I had learned

to address my Old Man Friend. *Why do you hesitate? You belong with my husband and me.*

My thinking to him caught him by surprise. He thought back to me, *hey, wait a minute. You aren't supposed to be able to sense me. I see they were right when they informed me you were a spirit too. This will be an interesting life. I will join you.*

When my husband came into the room, I told him we were having a tall son with blond hair. This was a big step for me. I told someone I had a psychic experience. An even bigger step for me was admitting to myself that it was real.

I would now tell my husband about what was happening. I was out of the closet, but the chicken in me would go no further than allowing my husband to know. No one else in my life could know.

Up to this point in my life, I had divided the world into the real and the unreal of my closet. Now I knew there was real and semi real. The two worlds operate side by side in my life. You see, I never did doubt my sanity. I did, however, doubt reality.

My birthdays are a good example of this. I have two birthdays. My real birthday is in November and puts me in my forties. (LOL. I started this book over twenty years ago. I am now in my sixties. It takes a long time to learn.) My other birthday falls in September. It is the day I died and started over again. My first birthday is real. My second birthday is semi real. It isn't pretend. It happened. The real world would have to make room for the semi-real world I was experiencing.

I began to look back at my life to see how real my semi-real world was. I pulled a memory from my closet of a time when I was sitting at the desk in my room, doing homework. I suddenly felt unhappy. I noticed the time on the clock as a reference point. I realized the feeling I was getting was the one I got when I found out what had happened. This is what it feels like to be psychic.

When I walked out to my car the next morning, I was unhappy to see a ticket on my window. The officer thought I had parked too close to the fire hydrant. The time on the ticket matched the time of my feeling.

That is what it's like to be psychic. It is a very fine, thin reality, but it is reality. It may be a reality that exists in my ability to sense it, but it is reality. If my Old Man Friend talks and only I hear him, does he still make a sound?

I was operating between two realities. I know the spirit isn't real, and neither is it pretending. I could also see how much of the real world was pretend. We are all so busy pretending that we are better than everyone else. We spend the rest of our time pretending we are all the same. We make up our minds about something, and that is the way it is. We never stop to think that it is that way only because we made it up that way. We are creating our reality.

Does reality exist only as far as we are able to perceive it? Is reality limited only by our ability to create it? Is the real reality waiting out there for us to discover it?

Did I lose you now? There is often confusion when putting things together. It is the chaos before the calm. That is how growing happens.

23

Blindsided by an Adversary

Life went on. I lived my little life centered on my husband and son. I was happy. I was seven years into my recovering from cancer and seeing heaven. I don't know which was more traumatic to me. They both affected me deeply. They both took some getting used to.

Little things happened that I shared with my husband, like when we were driving around and deciding which restaurant we wanted to stop at to eat dinner. I suddenly remembered a group of friends I knew in high school. My husband had never met them. I had played on the same basketball team with them. I knew them well. While still in the car, I began to tell my husband about some of the things my teammates and I had done. There appeared to be no reason for me to suddenly think about these people I hadn't seen in years. When we got into the restaurant, I saw my friends sitting there.

There was another time when I was sitting in the car, waiting for my husband. He was under the car's hood, checking the oil. I wanted to tell him to hurry because I didn't want to miss the beginning of the nine o'clock movie. I decided he wouldn't hear me. I kept my mouth closed. He stuck his head out and asked, "What did you say, honey?" I replied that I hadn't said anything. His answer surprised me because he said he had heard my voice. I swore I never opened my mouth; I was just thinking about it. He told me he had heard me and said I was doing "it" again.

The little things never got me upset. They were fun. The big things always threw me for a loop. I liked being surprised by seeing my old teammates at the restaurant. I didn't like being surprised by seeing an old adversary pop in on the night she died. I hadn't seen this person in years. I didn't know she was ill, yet there she stood in front of me in the middle of the night.

She had never been particularly nice to me when she was alive. I saw no reason to expect anything different just because she was now dead. Rosa was a friend of a friend, and we all hung out together. She tried to hide her dislike for me. She wasn't very good at it. I had two strikes against me as far as she was concerned. I wasn't Italian, and I came from the poor side of town.

There she stood in the middle of the night, uninvited and unwanted in my bedroom. She wanted to talk, and I didn't want to. I let her do all the talking. She came to clear up the differences between us. Now that she was on the other side, she could see things differently. She knew she had treated me unfairly. Rosa, the proud Italian, was asking me for forgiveness. I said I had always forgiven her each time she hurt me. She thanked me and was gone.

There I sat again, blindsided by the other side. What was I to make of this event? I couldn't ignore it and put it in my closet. When my husband woke up, I told him how upset I was.

Rosa's visit forced me to contend with the spirit. It isn't the fact that she visited me that upset me. It was the content of the meeting that upset me. Familiarity with the other side created an understanding that being psychic and having spirituality are the same thing. If I was to accept the psychic world, I must also accept the spiritual implications of its existence.

Feelings are real. There was no mistaking the feeling of remorse from Rosa. Feelings are very intense during stressful times. The added strength of a feeling during times of death and danger is what makes the psychic connection possible for those of us who are sensitive enough to perceive it. That is when the psychic world can break through to the real world. That is the reason deathbed visions are so common. The part of me that dissolved during my near-death experience was never totally restored. That is why I can see and feel so much more than I could before. I've become more sensitive.

When my Italian friend and I talked, it wasn't like we talked here on earth. On the other side, we only need to think to someone, and we become one. We met in the middle between her and me and become us. In the instant we communicated, I once again knew more than I wanted to. My reality once again was threatened by the bigger reality of the spirit world. I wished it would stop doing that.

I was having a hard enough time dealing with the reality of psychic experiences. I didn't want to enter the realm of spirituality. I was to learn later that being psychic is a side effect of being spiritual. In a world where words are necessary, the three words—*psychic, spiritual,* and *metaphysical*—can be interchanged in a sentence and still retain the same meaning. *God, Allah,* and *Supreme Being* can be interchanged in a sentence; it is only a matter of linguistics. The famous saying "A rose by any other name would still smell as sweet" means God by any name we call him would still be God.

How are you doing? I hope you are stepping into the closet with me. I have some really nice things to show you. It is a big closet.

_____

_____

24

A Different Other Side

My normal life continued. I was a normal human after all. I had to do dishes, go to work, and keep up on the shopping, just like all the other suburban mothers. No one suspected a thing about my closeted life. I liked it that way.

I was happy to once again find out I was pregnant. I waited to see the spirit that would come to join our family. I was confident that I would get prior knowledge once again. Nothing unusual was happening this time. My husband and I prepared the nursery and picked out names. This time we were having a girl, and Victoria was the name we chose.

It wasn't until the moment of her birth that I saw the spirit enter the baby's body. The first thing the spirit thought was, *my name is not Victoria.* This was one of the first times a spirit had to yell at me to get my attention. I found out that the spirit will come at its own time. The two children presented differently. I told my husband we needed to change the baby's name.

In that instant of greetings, I recognized her. She and I had been together many times, and we deeply loved each other. As she grew, she rebelled whenever I called her my daughter. She insisted she was *my* mother, and she made every attempt to treat me as her child. I was grateful when she grew out of this phase. She now calls me her mother.

This experience forced me to accept not only my spirit but also the fact that my spirit had a prior identity. I always knew that I had known my husband from before. I pulled the memory from my closet of what I knew of our relationship.

There was a time when I deeply hurt my husband by leaving him. It was in the lifetime when I was killed because of my psychic abilities. He felt that if I could just keep quiet about my gifts, then I wouldn't be found out and killed. I knew I had to use my talents to help others. I couldn't stop doing my mission any more than I could stop breathing.

There was also a more recent time when we were living on the frontier. He left to go hunting and never came back. I greatly mourned losing him. The more I experience the other side, the more I remember what I don't know. Each time I connect in any way with the spirit side of me, the connection grows stronger. I was still growing further and further away from being normal. I was gaining an understanding of living a psychic's life.

How do you identify what "it" is? Are you a psychic? Are you a spirit? Are you a mystic? Are you normal? Is it now normal to be "it"?

_____

_____

25

Not on My Side

I know some psychics claim to know it all. I don't make this claim. I never did learn to control what I see. The psychic world is bigger than I am. I don't control it.

I understand that many people experience knowing who will be on the other end of the line when the phone rings. They could do this even before the invention of caller ID. I could never do this. I tried, but it never worked for me.

I understand that it's very common to see people after they die. This I could do. I was used to it. I even expected it. My husband wasn't used to experiencing the psychic. He expected me to do so. Then one night he heard his father calling him, and he knew he had to go to the hospital. My father-in-law was currently in and out of the hospital. It was only a matter of time before cancer took his life.

My husband insisted on leaving at once. The urgency and speed of the two-hundred-mile drive allowed my husband to be with his family during this important time.

My husband could feel his father's need to have all his children there when he died. I didn't get the message addressed to my husband. This was a link of love between father and son. Psychic feelings and experiences can be faked, but there is no mistaking them when they are real. I didn't experience what my husband did, but I still believe it was real.

The moral of the story is that psychic experiences can be faked. They can be pretended, but there is no mistaking them when they are real. There are many Elvis impersonators. That doesn't mean that at some point an energy called "Elvis" never existed. It proves only that there was a great energy at one time, and others are trying to tap into it.

I won't pretend that I heard the message my husband received. I understand enough about the spirit world to know I don't know it all. You may not believe what I have to say, but I promise you that I won't pretend or lie.

Do you still wonder how this all works? Do you realize you too can do "it"?

26

Everything Changes

It was a night in October when my world changed. My husband was getting the children into their nightclothes. We were looking forward to watching the Garfield Halloween special and then going to bed.

My husband called for me from my daughter's bedroom. "Come look at this. Something is wrong with our daughter." When I looked at my daughter, I saw that her vaginal area had been injured. I called the police, and they escorted us to the hospital.

The doctors said she had been sexually assaulted. She was only three years old. How could anyone hurt my baby? The only time she had been away from me was while I was making dinner. I had heard the different children playing in my yard as I made spaghetti. They were out there for no more than an hour. I had thought she was safe in our own backyard.

The next day the police set up an interview with my daughter. Two ladies set up a camera in a room that looked like a typical living room. I wasn't allowed to be with her because my husband and I were the prime suspects. On the tape, she revealed who had hurt her. Two of the names I knew from the neighborhood. They were only children themselves. The third person she named was older. I have no idea who he or she is.

Those are the facts of the story, not the feelings. The feelings involve more, much more. When I was permitted to see the tape of my daughter, I watched in total silence, not moving a muscle. When it was over, I pulled my knees up, rolled into a ball, and cried. I was overwhelmed.

I didn't know what to do, but I knew I couldn't do anything the way my mother had. My family secret had taught me that lesson. My oldest sister had been the victim of incest. She also had been only a child when it started. She has had a very hard life as a result of this abuse. My mother? My mother said she never knew. My mother never did anything to help my sister. Mother only said my sister liked to make things up. She was no help to my sister. I think her reaction to the crime my father had committed hurt my sister more than the incest itself. I knew I must be there for my daughter. I couldn't fail her the way my mother had failed her children.

My mother lived in a different time. In the years when I was growing up, it was very hard to live without a man. I can understand why she had to keep her secrets. I can forgive her, but I cannot forget the results of her blindness when I see how my sister has suffered. I cannot allow my daughter to be condemned to the same shadowy life.

There are many things in life I have questioned. For me there was no question about the fact that I would stand by my daughter. There are many things in life I seek to understand. I will never understand how anyone could hurt a three-year-old.

What would you do in this situation? How would you go on?

27

Needing the Other Side

I hadn't been given a clue psychically about what would happen. I should have known. With all the things in my life I had foreseen. I should have foreseen this event and stopped it from happening. I felt so guilty. I now needed the skills of the other side.

With all the things I knew I could do, why couldn't I focus on the assailant and hurt him? I wanted to. If I had been skilled with the abilities I possess, I believe I would have known the meaning of the expression "all hell breaking loose." I was mad. I was irate. I was dangerous.

The person who had assaulted my daughter also took something from me. He took my innocence. I had grown up in the sixties and fought for peace. I was one of those hippies who believed in love. I now became a person who knew she could kill.

We began to receive strange phone calls. There were children chanting, "Ba ba ba best friends" on the other end of the line. Dead fish were thrown on our lawn. My husband reacted by punching his fist through the wall and buying guns. He bought me a pistol to always keep handy. There was also a shotgun. He said, "You don't even have to aim it. Just point it, and it will take out the door and anything else in the way." I knew I would use it if anyone tried to hurt my children ever again.

The world can talk all it wants about power and energy, but nothing matches the force of a mother protecting her young. Intense feelings can increase a psychic's ability. I was breaking phones and popping light bulbs left and right. I couldn't control it. My feelings were off the scale, and my closet became very accessible.

Have you ever lost control? Have you ever comforted someone who was handling a hardship? Have you ever not had any answers?

_____

_____

28

"It" Has Started

It had to eventually happen, that final moment when I would have to learn more about who and what I was, when there would be a definite decision to turn to my closet. Make no mistake about my motives when I entered the closet. I wanted to get the person who had hurt my daughter.

There is a turning point in everyone's life. Mine came when the cop looked at me and said, "Look, lady, there is nothing else we can do." There it was, that moment in time when everything stood still so all of time could pass in front of me. Thousands of thoughts flooded my mind in an instant. I looked back at the cop with a cold, determined stare and slowly said, "You don't know me."

I called out for my Old Man Friend. My spirit friend was never very far away. Over the years, I had ignored and neglected him, but he still occasionally checked up on me. I called out for help. He was there, as always.

I cried on his shoulder. He wrapped me in love. I asked him to help me get the person who had done this. He said he couldn't … unless I learned certain things first. I thought back to him with singular intent. "Then teach me!"

That did it. Those three little words would forever change my life. The door on the other end of my closet exploded off its hinges. A corridor was created for me. My decision had been made, and there was no turning back. I wanted punishment for the alleged assailant. I knew this was the way to get it. I was about to learn the real meaning of being a psychic.

Are you still with me? Will you come with me to the other side of my closet?

29

Starting a New Path

We sold our house in a great hurry. We needed to distance ourselves from the evil that had happened there. We moved into an available house. It wasn't the house I wanted. The house was exactly what I didn't want. I told myself it was only temporary and that we could move as soon as possible. Ten years later as I write this book, I find myself still in this house.

I had to be where I was for my life to unfold the way it did. I met a curious neighbor when I moved in. She was the type of woman my mother warned me about. She visited psychics to get readings. Her father had been a minister, so I knew she couldn't be too dangerous. We began to talk together. She introduced me to the other side.

What a sheltered life I had led! Here I was, thirty years old and going to my first psychic reading.

There was a traffic jam in front of us as we drove to the psychic's house. We were going to be late. I told my friend not to worry; it was a good day to do laundry, and the psychic would keep busy as she waited for us. As we pulled up in her driveway, I wasn't surprised to see freshly laundered sheets on the line outside her house.

She spread out the cards and started talking. She reminded me of my grandmother. The only difference was, I had never seen the same light around my grandmother that I saw around the room. The normal-looking psychic continued with the reading. There was nothing she said I didn't already know. Her gifts to me were showing and knowing it was safe to be psychic.

Where is your safety zone? My closet was my safety zone. Can your safety zone include the other side of the closet?

_____

_____

PART 4

Confessions of School

30

Easy Street

Life had been easy up to this point in my life. It was easy because I had this psychic ability that always gave me the answers. I now realize that life was easy because I always took the easy way out. Things were about to change.

Earlier in my life, all I had to do was think a question, and I had an answer come to me. Now when I looked at my daughter, I had no idea what to do, where to go, or how to help her. I had to learn. But what was it I had to learn? For the first time in my life, I had no answers.

My Old Man Friend was there, as always. He had the answer. He told me it wouldn't be easy. I knew exactly what he meant. You see, I had been around my friend long enough to know what he was about.

I pulled another memory from my closet of a time when I was recovering from one of my surgeries. Fluid had built up in my lungs, and breathing was a problem. My Old Man Friend instructed me not only on how to breathe but also on what to think as I breathed. He said I must breathe deeply of God's gift of clean air. I was told to picture life coming into me as I inhaled. Even further he reminded me to get rid of the bad that had accumulated inside me. With each breath out, I knew in my mind that I was pushing out what had no place in me.

Picture this if you can. I was in the hospital, weak and tired. My Old Man Friend showed up and started acting like a personal trainer, yelling at the top of his lungs (as if he had any), "One, two, three, four, five … Come on, girl, stay alive!"

It isn't that I wanted to die. It just hurt to breathe deeply. It was all I could do to breathe the short, shallow breaths required for life. The simple act of expanding my chest exhausted me. My Old Man Friend encouraged me to breathe in for a count of five, then I exhaled, so grateful to be done.

This exercise went on for some time. "In with the good air, out with the bad." When the small coughs interrupted the rhythm of breathing, my Old Man Friend congratulated me and said, "Each cough expels more of that which should not be, pushing it further and further away from thee."

My Old Man Friend often had the annoying habit of thinking in rhymes. He also needed to include God in whatever he was teaching me. My private tutor also spoke of things that came from Eastern religions. I didn't know it at the time. My friend was teaching me a visualization to assist in healing myself.

This is what it's like to live with a spirit guide. Living with him for as many years as I had, I became accustomed to his style. I once excused away his oddities as a facet of his personality. I later realized this spirituality was the very core of his being. I was fortunate enough to be able to hear my spirit guide. I was even more fortunate to have been able to learn from him.

I knew all too well what he meant when he said learning wouldn't be easy. The easy part of my life was over. If I were going to progress in life, I would have to work at it.

Now, as my Old Man Friend stood before me and offered me a chance to go to a new school, I knew all too well what this also meant. My Old Man Friend was saying goodbye. I reluctantly agreed. I was never so happy in my life or so sad. I knew my Old

Man Friend was right to send me away. I knew he was right because he always was.

School was going to make a difference. School was going to make me different. My Old Man Friend introduced me to a new guide, a guide in a new land, a guide on the other side of my closet. I didn't know what I was getting myself into. I also knew I must go. I had to make my Old Man Friend proud.

Thank you for staying with me. The next part was hard work for me to write. It will be easy for you to listen.

31

New Land

I was a stranger in a strange land. The other side of my closet was uncharted territory. I was grateful my Old Man Friend had found me such a wonderful guide.

The man in whose hands I was placed was known to me as the Leader. The Leader made it perfectly clear that I was no longer in charge. When you go into an unknown land, you don't hire a guide and then tell your guide where to go. The Leader would take me in the direction I needed to go.

On earth, the Easterners call this "letting go of the ego." This is what we Westerners fear the most. I am a born and bred Westerner. I not only feared letting go; I thought it was a folly. Was I making a mistake by listening to the spirits only I could hear? At this point in my life, it didn't matter. I had hit rock bottom. I needed to know how to help my daughter, and I didn't care where the help came from. The school bell had rung. Classes were about to begin.

The mechanics of the school in the sky were very simple. I went to school while I slept. I know about dreams. This wasn't a dream. If it was a dream, it was a very long dream because it lasted about three years. Each morning when class ended, my homework assignment was acted out during the following day. Each night as I returned to class, the lesson continued. Periodically my day was interrupted by a "Time for a lesson, my child," at which point I became tired and needed a short nap. It was then that I found myself once again back in school.

School in the sky was very much like school on earth with a few exceptions. Class was held outside in a beautiful cove. The setting itself was very nourishing. I mean, the pristine beauty was literally feeding me. There was, however, one big difference. Instead of a solitary moon moving in the night sky, three orbs danced their way across a fully lit sky. I had to face the fact that I was no longer in Kansas and that my school was somewhere in the sky.

Did you ever travel to other countries? Did you notice the changes?

_____

_____

32

New Deal

I remembered my deal with myself to no longer put things in my closet. Where could I put what was happening now? When I accepted being psychic, the boundaries of reality changed. Now, as I stepped into the world of spirituality, the boundaries of time collapsed. I felt like I was playing poker with a stacked deck. The cards were stacked in my favor so I couldn't lose, but as each card was flipped, it was as if I already knew what would be next.

What kind of deal could I make with myself now? I wanted and needed to know who had hurt my daughter. I knew my secret side was the only means I had to get answers. I couldn't turn away from my source, and I also couldn't fully embrace it. This school was not only far away; the whole thing was farfetched.

I am a very human spirit and a very adventurous soul. I didn't know what was going to happen. I just didn't want to miss any of it. I went off to school with mixed feelings. I was excited about learning and scared of knowing. Knowing my secrets had been fun when I was little. I somehow knew the mysteries that lay ahead. I didn't want to deal with any of it.

The human part of me is a realist. (Imagine me using the term *realist* to apply to myself.) I decided to treat this new school just like I had treated college. That would mean two things. One, I would work hard and study. Two, I was going to have fun.

I put myself through college here on earth. I worked during the day and went to school at night. This new school would have to take a back seat to my human life. I carried on with my daily life and went to school at night. None of this seemed strange to me. I felt like I belonged at school and somehow remembered being there before.

When I went to college on earth, I learned the importance of taking good notes. I began to keep a log of what I was learning at night school. Just like in college, I also had to conduct further research outside of class. I had another motive for doing research. I am human. I didn't trust them.

A higher education is important. This school was the next step I was searching for. It was the new generation thought starting.

33

New Friend

I met other interesting beings about this time. My Old Man Friend was keeping his word. He would teach me about the spirit. There is an expression that states, "When the student is ready, the teacher will appear." I know this isn't true. The teacher is always there, waiting. We must become ready to learn. I was ready to learn.

My Old Man Friend had friends. George is about as normal as they come. He was a steady, calming being. They don't come any smoother than George. George didn't like to talk too much. He would just hang around the house and be. He had no direction or mission that I could discern. My Old Man Friend always had a reason for coming to see me. He always came to help by teaching me the mysteries of life. George wasn't at all like my Old Man Friend; I don't know how they were friends, but they were.

In looking back with the wisdom that comes only with future knowledge, I know now what he was. George was the first step, the first lesson. George simply was. He was peace. He had nothing on his agenda. He simply was.

When he was near, I would slow down and just be. This felt very much like the time I had my NDE, when you experience such peace because you are unconditionally loved. There is no judgment. On earth the sentence "I love you" is often followed by the suffix *if* or *but*. George radiated "I love you"—period, end of sentence, and nothing else needed to be added.

George was a great blessing to me. He calmed me down. I needed to be calmed down. I was an emotional wreck. My daughter was going through some rough times. I had to be strong for her. My little girl had hidden her Bert and Ernie dolls in the back of the closet. They were boy dolls, and she wanted nothing to do with them. The three-year-old who had spoken full sentences at an early age began to stop talking.

What was I to do? The answers that had always come to me so easily were now silent. Most of my days were spent waiting for the night. At night I could cry in the shower, and no one knew. I also started night school. My Old Man Friend was right in sending me to night school.

George became an intermediary between the two worlds. He had lived a more recent life on earth and could translate a lesson into a modern setting so it had more relevance to me. He could take the most complex subject and break it down to be more manageable. George was simple and unassuming. He was smooth. He was the exact opposite of me.

I had a rebellious streak in me. I thought I knew all the answers for myself. Up to this point in my life, rebelling against things I didn't agree with had worked well for me. It had kept me intact. It had kept my world intact. But things were different now. My world was no longer intact.

Changes in your life will change you, and my whole world

had been shattered. My natural rebellion kept me intact when I was living in a dysfunctional family. "An irrational response to an irrational world will still bear irrationality," George reminded me.

George created a story in my head. Communication with a spirit is often done with a picture that tells a thousand words. He replayed sections of my life for me. All I could see in these sections was what was happening to me. I still didn't get it.

George needed to translate for me. Into my head, he played another scenario. I saw a family with members who all lived together. The father of the family had a birth defect that made him limp. The children of the family didn't have the birth defect, but they all had the limp because they thought that was the way to walk. By the time the children were older, they had damaged their bodies by walking in this odd fashion. Most of the children stayed close to home because of the ridicule they felt when they went into the world. One of the offspring looked out into the world and wondered what it would be like to be different. She occasionally ventured out and then retreated to the safety of her family. Even if her family was a little distorted, it was home to the little girl.

As time and fate would have it, she eventually stayed away from home more and more and eventually made it to the world that didn't limp. Then this growing girl fell in love with a man who limped (he had addictions like alcoholism). She married him and started her own family. As her children grew, she noticed her children starting to limp.

George stopped his story and asked me to finish it for myself. I understood that I was this girl who limped. I understood the cycle would perpetuate itself if I didn't change. I understood I had asked for this crisis in my life to accentuate the problem I couldn't identify. I knew the problem, but I didn't know the answer.

"That is why you also asked to have us, your friends on the other side, with you. That is why you are sent to school," George answered. I knew this had a double meaning. I knew George meant both what is known in the earth school and my private school in the sky. There in my head was a picture of parallel roads that kept intersecting repeatedly. Each time the roads intersected, I felt the desire to turn in a new direction only to lead away down the familiar path of going in the same direction.

George continued his teaching by showing me another picture in response to my picture. At the next intersection, there came along a slight breeze that caught my attention. I enjoyed the cool, fresh breeze. I continued in the direction I had always taken before. At each intersection, my friend George made the breeze stronger and stronger until it literally knocked me off my feet.

I had no choice at this point in picture exchanges but to pick myself up, dust myself off, and suddenly realize I had no idea in which direction I was headed. I was lost.

George is the exact opposite of me in all but one important exception. He is just as stubborn and determined as I am. He wouldn't give up on me in this lifetime or in the others. That is one of the interesting things about what I have discovered about the other side that also holds true on this side.

You will become very much like those you spend time with. George's simple and unassuming ways taught me to be more open to his kind and loving ways. My family's harsh and twisted way of thinking also trapped me in a cycle that continues with harsh thinking. I do love my family, but I don't love being with them.

I love George. I do love what I become when I am with him. It is my life. It is my choice. I choose to change.

Are you waiting for the next shoe to drop? Do you wonder what will come next? Buckle up, the ride will get rough.

34

A Friend Visits

For every three steps taken forward, I took one step back and looked at what was happening. I was learning not only to enter their world but also how their world merged with ours.

The door to the other side swung both ways. I could enter their world and go to school. They too could enter my world. I was used to my Old Man Friend coming to counsel me. I loved him dearly, and he always helped me in a way only a true friend would. Now, some of my teachers from school were popping in and coaching me.

I stepped back and examined this new issue in my life. I not only heard the voices of my new friends, but I could also see one of them sitting next to me in the car.

I will have to tell you another story here. I was minding my own business, driving to the bookstore to get a book to research some school project. Next to me popped in Alton. "You know, this whole trip will be to your chagrin," he said.

What? It annoys me when friends stop by without an invitation. It really upsets me when they use words I don't know.

When I got to the bookstore, I went straight to the dictionary section. I was going to "chagrin" him. I tried to look up the word but couldn't find it. I didn't know how to spell *chagrin*. Walking over to the checkout, I asked the lady behind the counter to help me. After some work together, we finally found the definition. It meant I would be not only disappointed but also upset about being disappointed.

Well! What did Alton know anyway? I went off to find the book I had originally come in for, but I couldn't find it. The kind lady behind the counter said they had just sold out of it. I was disappointed. But I wasn't upset about it, at least not that upset. I browsed around the store and found another book that caught my attention. Later that night, when I settled down to do some relaxing reading, I had another surprise. There on page five of the book was a sentence using the word *chagrin*.

Did you ever have an acquaintance who became a good friend after a short time? That is why I call them "friends," not "guides."

35

Alton

Since I already mentioned him, I may as well introduce you to Alton. Alton is the spirit I saw and heard in the car. Alton is also one of the teachers from my school in the sky. Alton is a spirit of many words. George rarely talks, but Alton, oh Alton. Alton always has something important to say. At the end of a lesson, Alton will recapitulate the lesson within a well-constructed sentence.

Alton is a writer. When you are with his spirit, you immediately think of ancient Greece. Alton isn't ancient. You don't have shoulders like that if you are ancient. It would be fair to say Alton carries himself well.

Alton is a word wizard. He can paint a picture with words that can truly help you see what he sees, feels what he feels, and be what he is. His lessons are always short and compact. "You should never waste words by expounding where it is not necessary," he would say.

"When you start to rattle on, you begin to be like the empty gourd that has lost all its meat and all that is left is the seed. Think first of what you want to say and then say it without distracting yourself or the reader."

He is a very thorough teacher. With a teacher like him, is it any wonder that I feel I must write all this down in a book? As I write a chapter, he intercedes when I start to get off the theme. "Get back to the plot, or you will get lost out there," he advises. "Let the student do the thinking. You do the writing," he prompts.

He knows what he is doing. He will construct a plot and give only enough to allow the student to learn the lesson. "You must learn it yourself, or it is not yours."

Oh, would that I could
Give you all the answers.
Oh, would that I could
Make everything right.

Oh, how you struggle
And sometimes fail.
Oh, how you grow and
Then try once more.

Oh, would that you could
Make everything fit just so.
Oh, would that it could be
As I guide and guard.

Oh, would that you could
Have my joy
When I see you
Finally get it right.

When you finally realize
It's not what you thought,

Then I see you have learned
What cannot be taught.

You must do it and live it.
It is hard fought.
You must make it real,
Or it is only a passing thought.

All for now.

That is how each class ends. No class dismissed, no ringing bell.
The simple statement "all for now" promises more to come.

Does Alton sound real? Do you now see how real the other side is?
Would you like to meet more of my friends?

36

Lewadanna

What would school be without classmates? I must introduce a special being. She gets special billing. She wasn't one of the teachers. She was just another student. That is why we became such good friends. Her name was Lewadanna. I'm not sure I am spelling it right, and neither was she. She said that when she lived on earth, they wrote differently. They didn't use the same language used in my time. The essence of her being spoke of a time that was before anything I could use as a reference point. The land she was a part of was one of the Americas. Again, neither she nor I was sure which one. Each student was asked to stand and give a short introduction of himself or herself.

Building was her trade. She was from the time of making buildings and temples. She was involved in the construction of cities and cultures. "My people learned to work together to create something that would last longer than any of us will," she said with pride. "My people make buildings, buildings that are as big as our people. We are united to be strong."

"Today I am asked to tell you about walls. Not the kind of walls that separate you from anything else. I speak of the walls we build. The right kind of wall to build isn't determined by which is the best wall possible. The right wall is determined by what is necessary. I wouldn't use the mighty walls of the temple for where I live. I'm not important. My home won't need to endure."

She knew the building business. I was certain of that. Times were certainly different in her time. The Leader thanked Lewadanna for her contribution to the class, and she took her place among the other students. "Now class," the Leader continued, "let us see what the walls can teach us.

"Your worlds are like the walls. Some of your worlds operate like the plank walls. There are members of your society who serve as beams. The beams are stronger and can support the planks to create the walls. Wood is what you have, so wood is what you use. The same is true for a thatch hut or a tepee.

"There is another type of world you live in where conformity is important. This is when you build your society with bricks. It matters not if the bricks are chiseled from stone or baked in an oven. Conformity is important. The mortar, the stuff of spirit, is what holds it all together, not the stronger piece of wood that pulls it together but something totally different.

"Yet we know of another wall or society that accepts all forms of stones. The fieldstones are also held together by spirit. Each society will be different. A canyon stone wall is beautiful and enduring.

"The binding force that works through you and in you and for you will hold together the society you make."

Lewadanna and I knew the leader was implying the "all," the spirit, the piece of God that binds different worlds. I was grateful to have another student in class with me I could identify with.

Does your mind wander as you get a piece of a class? Do you know it isn't wandering—it is growing?

_____

_____

37

Broken Boundaries

Confessions are hard to tell. They are even harder to tell when you make a mistake. When you are new to something, you don't do things right the first time or two.

I have another story for you. Before I get started, I will let you know there will be many interpretations. There will be those among you who will simply call me a liar. Others will claim I am making it all up. The learned among you will debate whether I'm a multiple personality or someone who is simply schizophrenic. The religious among you will claim I am possessed. The spiritual will recognize this as channeling. I call it "when me and thee make we."

When you, the reader, see, hears, or feel anything, it is necessary to put the information into a context that can be related to. Each of us will make up different stories according to what our experiences are. We reveal much more about ourselves when we put forth an interpretation than we do about the subject at hand. When I tell you some of my secrets, what you make of them will reveal what you are and very little of what I am.

"Is the glass half full or half empty?" Your answer will reveal much about you and nothing about what the glass is all about. If you really want to know something, you must go to the source. "If you ask the glass," my friends suggest, "you will get the correct answer." Now I talk to my friends, but I draw the line at talking to glasses. I know all things are alive with energy. I will not talk to glasses. The answer can be correct only if you hang out with the glass long enough to know whether the glass is in the process of emptying or filling up. I want to know about the glass, not about me.

Please, dear readers, reserve all your ideas and comments until the end of this story. Please don't read anything into it. Just accept me for what I am. It's hard not to judge me. It is even harder for me to reveal these things about myself. Maybe if you put yourself in my place the way you would put yourself in the glass's place, then you will see why revelations are so hard. Story time once again. I hope I don't confuse you by always stopping to tell you stories, but as Alton says, "Everyone loves a good story."

Well, enough putting this off. I will just have to tell you the story. I admit I'm not an expert. I knew nothing about the other side of my closet. I knew nothing about how it would enter back to the earth side of the closet. I was in uncharted territory. I had no schooling in this area. Where could I go to learn about this even if I wanted to? I made a few mistakes along the way. Some mistakes, in retrospect, will seem funny. Others will be downright hilarious, even as they happen.

When I first started to communicate with my friends, I could do so only while I was asleep. Just before falling asleep, I felt this floating feeling, then a tingling, and then a greeting. "Greetings, little one." That is the way it worked. It all sounds simple, right? It was simple when things went right, but sometimes things didn't go right. Let me explain.

I often took afternoon naps because my day job started early in the morning. It was during one of these naps when I was suddenly interrupted. My daughter ran into the house, announcing that she must go to the mall right away because she needed a white turtleneck for a school performance tomorrow. "All right, all right, let's get into the car and go," I said to her.

I heard one of my unseen friends yell, "Wait. I haven't disconnected yet."

"Well then, get out of here" was my reply to him.

"I cannot unless you are in the right state," he explained to me.

Really now! I thought back to him. *I don't have the time for this. You are just going to have to come with us. I can't take a nap right now.*

I had channeled before, but this was the first time we had gone out together. As I was driving, my unseen friend was amazed by what he was seeing.

"All these cars know where they are going. They shoot about without bumping into each other," he observed.

"Yes, most of the time we don't bump into each other," I explained as I rolled my eyes.

"Well, it is a wonder you don't bump more often" was his reply.

When we all finally safely reached the mall and went inside, my unexpected guest exclaimed, "Why did you not tell me we were going to the marketplace?" We went from store to store as my friend was having a grand old time looking at everything. Suddenly I heard my friend exclaim, "I smell onions. I love onions. Let us stop and get onions." I looked up, and there was a Coney Island. Nothing would do, but we stopped in for a little snack.

I have since learned how to properly channel my friends. I tell you this only because I don't wish to take credit for the things they do. The only thing I will take credit for is being such a good channel that very few people can tell when I am doing it. If you examine my writings, some of you will be able to tell the difference between their writing and mine. This gives whole new meaning to the term *ghostwriting*, does it not?

Did you see the two sides merging in this story? Does it make you wonder?

38

The Joker

There was another friend who insisted on being known. "Center stage is where I belong," he often reminded me. The Joker had an accent I attribute to the South Seas. His occupation was in a questionable field. He liked to call himself an entertainer. I agreed with him there. He was very entertaining.

He was the master of the one-liners. Alton's quotes are always enlightening. The Joker's quotes are always funny. I once asked the Leader why we tolerate such behavior. His answer was that the joker served his purpose. "Humor is a tool that will allow you to address issues that are too sensitive to examine in any other way."

In retrospect and with love, I now know what his purpose was. The Joker was a groundbreaker and ground shaker. When I was up against an unshakable truth, he shook me up with some funny comment to bust the idea apart. To others it might have appeared that he was misbehaving, and I agree with you there, but he was so funny and harmless.

Let me give you an example. I was sitting in a discussion group with a self-imposed know-it-all. This learned man could quote this and that to support all his beliefs. When my friend had had enough of some of the expert's comments, I channeled his one-line response: "Well, that makes as much sense as 'because I said so,'" I laughed. The Joker laughed. The other people in the group laughed. The expert? He wasn't laughing.

The Joker has a very important gift to share with us. He is extremely necessary to life. He gives us laughter. I love to have fun. I love when he is around. I love what his laughter does for me.

The Leader was right when he said the Joker serves a purpose. Laughter can work where reason fails. My Leader reminded me that there are two ingredients necessary for laughter. The first that is necessary is accepting something. The second necessary ingredient is rejecting that very same thing. In that moment of noticing how ridiculous something is, you are free to laugh instead of just going along with the crowd. I love to laugh.

Do you want to learn more? Do you feel yourself opening?

_____

_____

39

Cross Checking

My private school in the sky both confirmed and conflicted with the research I was conducting during my waking hours. Crystals were the latest thing. Everywhere you turned, there was another book, class, or article about these beautiful items. I went to school and asked for input on the matter. The leaders obliged by bringing forward a teacher to assist in my learning.

Those who are saying crystals have power are remembering a time when they truly did. Just as in your time, oil has power. Power, my child, is nothing without the knowledge of how to use it. The knowledge of how to use the crystals gave power to the possessor of the crystal. Further, you must know now that even knowledge is nothing without the understanding of proper usage. And understanding? Understanding is but an offshoot of wisdom. And wisdom? Wisdom is only a starting point.

Another teacher came to the front and brought forth another view. "The power that you attribute to the crystal is the power you give it. As you focus on the healing properties of the crystal, you are but using the crystals, an extension of your own. You still have much to learn of the abilities you possess."

Yet another teacher graced the sands with a presence that had the other teachers step back. When she lifted her head to speak, her beauty amazed me.

"And yet I shall speak of the nature of things. I will teach you what nature will reveal about itself so you will see it in you too, my child. For you are very much like the crystals. The first thing you must know about crystals is that they grow. The very size, shape, and color depend on the environment that nourished it. The same for you, my child.

"Crystals are part of a cluster. If you wish to examine only one, you must break it away from the rest of the group. Not all crystals can be separated from their source. Some cannot be on their own because they didn't develop enough of their own separateness. For now, let us examine the single specimen to see what it can reveal to us.

"This crystal has five sides. When you hold a crystal and look inside, what you will see is through to the other side. It is as if the crystal is allowing you to see the world through the inner thoughts of the crystal. One of the sides will allow you to see through to the other, but everything will be magnified. Another side will create a view that is very murky, hard to understand, and hard to see through. Another side will allow you to see things just as they are. No change, just accepting things as they are. There are many sides to crystals and many sides to you also, my child.

"Can you see now how the crystals are much like you? Can I now show you more of you? When I look at you, my child, from my perch high above, I see another view of what you are made of. Look now, my little one, from up above to the object you wish to learn of.

"The tip of a crystal will have seven facets. These facets won't all be equal in size. Some of the facets of the crystals and your life will take up more than half of what you are. Some of the facets will be so small that you will have a hard time even finding them. But even the small facets change the tilt of the larger facets. You are too, my child, with your life as it is with the crystals.

"There is one more thing I want you to learn from the crystals. One more thing the crystal will reveal about itself that you will find true about yourself. The crystal has only one point. That one point is also in you. I ask you now to look inside yourself and find the point of your life using each of the wonderful sides of yourself and the different facets of your being. All for now."

Waking up in the real world was going to be tough this morning. I had to hurry to write all this down before I forgot it all.

Have you just met my ladies? The two of them are always together. Like harmony, they fit well together so the sound is beautiful. There was also a crystal I have since lost that was a natural crystal. It did have five sides. Most of the crystals you find in stores are manufactured and cut to be the same. What do you think about that?

_____

_____

40

Questions

I was questioning everything. I questioned what my new teachers taught and looked for verification in books on earth. I questioned what was taught on earth and looked for answers from my friends and teachers in school. I questioned myself to see just how much of this I should accept.

I questioned. *When did all this start? Why was it happening to me? How does all this work? Why does it all work? Who am I? Who are you? Why are we here? Why are you here? Why are you there?*

I went to school to get answers.

One question was foremost on my mind. My daughter. What was I to do to help her? The child who had spoken early began to stop talking. There wasn't a night that went by when I didn't find her sleeping on the floor next to my bed when I woke up. Getting her to sleep was difficult until I explained that I still had my pistol. I would protect her if that bad man came again.

For every question, there is an answer. Many of my questions had many answers because the other side had multiple spirits willing to help. Then I lay myself down to sleep, waiting for the answer I sought.

"Greetings once again, my child. It is good to be with you again. You ask yourself, 'Why we?' Your friends are here. We are here because you have invited us. You are a part of us. We couldn't leave you any more than your hand could leave your body. The only way you could do this is if you cut it off. Cutting off your hand would be distorting part of you. You wouldn't hurt yourself or us in this manner.

"Today we will help you with some of your questions. Your Bible tells you to only ask, and it will be given to you. A question is the method by which you call us. We hear your private pondering during your busy day. You ask so many questions.

"Do you know what a question does to you? Do you know how a question looks to us? Your mind is like a chalkboard. During your waking hours, the board is full of ideas and writings. There is so much going on in your mind that it is hard for even yourself at times to understand all that has been written in your thoughts. When you meditate or sleep, it is like an eraser has cleared the board so there is room for us to give you answers.

"Mankind is so busy thinking their thoughts that they rarely have time to listen. The thoughts get so tangled up that there is no understanding them. That is the reason you need to sleep. During your sleep, your mind (spirit) can make sense of what your brain (body) has done during the day. There is a basic data dump that then gets classified and stored so that retrieval can be achieved. Sleep is needed so that you can understand yourself better. When you don't get enough sleep, your brain and body will suffer.

"We come to you when you meditate or sleep because there is room for us. Ask your questions my little one. We will help you with the things you need. Ask your questions and then wait for an answer. Don't fill up the silence with your own thoughts, for then we cannot get through to you. It is like your telephone. We get a busy signal and must try again later.

"We can come to you during your quiet times. That is when the channels open between our two worlds. When you question, there is a blank spot for us to enter. When you sleep, you have no choice but to listen to us. When you meditate, the conversations between the two worlds are more easily retrievable. When you stop talking, you can listen. When you close your eyes, you can see.

"Question all things, my child. Question us too. Ask and it will be given to you. All for now."

Can you see how this works? Can you now do "it" too?

41

Teaching a Name

Learning names on the other side is different from learning names on this side. My Old Man Friend is named exactly what he is. He is an old man, and he is my friend. Alton and George simply introduced themselves, and therefore they have regular names. The Leader, my Leader, was introduced to me as "the Leader," so that is what I have always called him.

Names on the other side are more like Indian names. Indian names have meanings. That is why my ladies are called "my ladies" and my Leader is called my "Leader" and especially why the Joker is called the "Joker."

There comes a time when names aren't enough. The Leader, my Leader, worked for and deserves his name. He encompasses all the qualities of being a leader. He was beginning to encompass more than being a leader. We had been together many times. I enjoyed his lesson and the love I could feel feeding my very soul. He was more than a leader. He was more than my leader. He was my friend.

One night, while sitting in our cove, I looked up at him and asked, "By what shall I call you, dear Leader?"

Call me that which you do, he thought back to me.

I stood up and said further to him, "But dear Leader, that doesn't seem like enough. I wish to know what you wish to be known as."

Then the pictures began to play in my head. It was as if he had taken out his wallet, and the flip-flop of all the pictures continued for miles and miles.

I looked at him and said, "Dear Leader, I only wanted your name, and you give me all this?"

"No, my little one," he started to reply. "You asked what I am to be known as, and I simply showed you."

I now call him "the Leader," "my Leader," "dear Leader." I cannot remember his full name.

Can you feel a closeness with the Leader? A leader you don't follow but a leader you wish to emulate.

42

Teaching the Spirit

The hardest part of listening to my friends is translating what they are saying. They carry with them an odd way of thinking and talking. They are a product of the times in which they lived. Their manner of speech is reflective of this. Sometimes the "thee and thou" really got to me. I thought to myself that if they wanted to be relevant, they must become current. I have a hard time following them and their examples when I must translate what they are teaching.

They must have been listening. The next class started with, "And now we shall teach a lesson using your Beatles." I thought I was hearing them wrong. The picture in the class was of the singing group, not the insect.

Wow, they do listen to me, I thought as I made a mental note to start watching what I was thinking.

The lesson consisted of appreciating the individual talents that work together to make a greater whole. Each Beatle contributed an element that congealed together to make the group. The members didn't always get along. Each soul at times rubbed the other soul the wrong way. But for a while, they worked together and created the Beatles. "You are what you are for a while, and when you are done, you change your style," my writing coach added in.

The Beatles also did what all things must do. They ended. Each soul did what it did and needed to do other things. All things, all souls, must grow and change. All for now.

There it was again, "all for now"; the lesson had ended. They know when my wakefulness will interrupt the lesson. They put it on hold for the next night. I can expect the lesson to be absorbed and used in my life in the next few days. This is their equivalent of homework. The next time class continues, the lesson picks up where they left off.

"Yes, little one [This was their usual method of addressing me]. You have applied the lesson of the Beatles. Their togetherness created the whole, and their individuality made it impossible for them to continue. Each soul had its own path and purpose. Mourn no more for what has passed. Revel in the creation of the new step as one gives way to the next.

"All for now, little one."

I hadn't asked for this lesson. My friends knew I was grieving the death of a friend. I felt such anguish for the two children she had left behind. Their words gave me comfort that night instead of answers. After all, what are friends for?

Have you ever worked with people who became good friends? That is how it works in spirit too.

_____

_____

43

Fancy Words

When I was still a little girl, the wise words of others meant nothing to me. My inexperienced mind couldn't yet understand what others were trying to teach me.

When I was young, I lost a precious toy. I searched the house and couldn't find it. My mother said, "Don't worry. It will be found in the last place you look."

Finally, I knew where to look. I figured it must be under my brother's bed because after that I would look no further. I ran to his room and peered under his bed, and to my surprise, the toy wasn't there.

I don't get this, I thought. I looked under my other brother's bed. I was certain it would be under there because I really would look no farther after that. There under my other brother's bed was absolutely nothing.

This told me only one thing. My mother didn't know what she was talking about. I was annoyed. Even as a little girl, I had little patience. I continued to look for my toy. Eventually, I found it. When my mother saw me playing with my toy, she asked me where I had found it. "In the basement" was my answer.

"That must have been the last place you looked then," my mother replied.

I got it. I understood what she had meant all along. How come I didn't get it earlier? I remember that lesson even to this day. The moral of the story isn't to keep looking until you find what you need. The moral of the story isn't even "Everything has a place. Everything should be in its place," as I have heard my mother say so often. The moral of the story for me is, I had a lot to learn, and while I was learning, I was unaware I was learning until I finally got it.

Alton often gives wise words to remind me of a lesson. But his quotes can only reinforce what I already know. Until I live a lesson, the wise words mean nothing to me.

Learning from wise words still gives me a problem. I love to read from the book *A Course in Miracles*, but I can tolerate only small doses of this rich material. Life would be much better if such material were required reading and even better if it somehow required understanding. Life, however, isn't like that. We must learn things the hard way the way I did as a small child. I was given the answer. I just didn't get it until I lived it. That is why we are here.

There it is. Another answer to another of my questions. I had asked the question weeks ago. This is a good time to dispel another fallacy of being psychic. It takes time. There is a sudden light that will descend on you and give you wisdom. This is a gift. You must do the work to make yourself ready to receive the gift. This takes time. There again is another answer to "Why are we here?" We are here because it takes time. Time doesn't exist on the other side, so they must come here to experience it.

I had asked a barrage of questions. Little by little, my friends were answering them. There was one big question they always stayed away from. Whenever I asked about my daughter's assailant, they answered, "In time, child, in time."

I was peeved every time I heard this. "What do you know about time anyway?" I mumbled to myself as if I didn't know they were listening.

Once you become friends, do you feel you can be a little sassy? It works in spirit also.

_____

_____

44

Do a Two-Step

Learning to dance takes a lot of time. When I was still a little girl, someone tried to teach me to tap dance. They stood in front of me and showed me how to do the heel toe. I mirrored their actions and got good at this heel-toe stuff.

Then they said I would have to do a heel-toe step. *OK, I can handle this*, I thought. It was beginning to make sense because I could hear the rhythm of my feet as they moved across the floor. I was pleased with my progress.

Then the instructor introduced me to heel, toe, step, and shuffle. This was getting a little harder. I had to concentrate and practice, or I would trip over my feet and mess things up.

Life is a lot like dancing. There is a lot to learn and practice. We will make mistakes and mess up. We will keep practicing until we finally get it right. We will know it inside when we finally get it right. We will be able to do the steps like they are second nature to do, because then and only then will they be part of us.

When we are finally good at doing our steps, we will be given harder steps to do. But to get the dance right, we must do all the steps, and we must practice until we get them right, or they will show in our actions.

We humans have become afraid of one of the steps necessary to do the dance of life. The judgment part of life is feared and ignored. We haven't been shown the correct way to do the judgment step. Judgment is a two-step process. Judgment must also be followed by acceptance.

Once again, I time-jumped into my near-death experience. I recognized this lesson as the next feeling I encountered on my journey back home. The life review is followed by the most delicious sense of understanding another side I have ever encountered. It feels better than an orgasm.

My dance instructor on the other side called himself Thomas. Thomas was the first spirit who had feet. The reason I noticed his feet was because he had an odd habit of pacing back and forth in front of the class as he spoke. There was a dance-like quality to his movements. His feet could keep rhythm to the message of the lesson. The pace would quicken when his stories were streaking out of him like a wildfire seeking more to burn. Slowing down and searching the sky with his eyes as if all our answers were out there somewhere, he could use his hands to add enriching dimensions to the plot. And when he turned to face us and paused just for a moment, we knew the next thing out of his mouth would be substantial. Oh, what a teacher! What a showman!

Thomas's expertise was the Bible. He lived and breathed the Bible. That is the reason both he and the Bible came alive whenever he spoke of it. The first lesson he taught was the first lesson from the good book. "We should start at the beginning, should we not, my students?" he began. He sounded like my tap teacher. He didn't look anything like her.

The first steps were taken across the sands as he moved with purpose and intent. "When we first meet the greatest teacher, we see him in the act of creating. Our Father is making that which will be."

Thomas proceeded by recapitulating the story of Genesis. The assignment to the class was to examine the story and see what we could learn from it.

"Think now, my students, that when God had finished with his work of creation, he looked and saw it was good." Thomas paused and turned, waiting for the impact of the words to hit us. "God examined his work and thought it was good." He continued as his thoughts and pace quickened. "He judged. Now I don't expect all of you to be able to say your work is good right off. Maybe down the line, when you are more skilled, you will be able to say such a thing." My teacher purred as he reached out his arm to try to touch some forward time we needed to aim for. Slowing down and looking into each pair of our eyes, Thomas continued, "But for now, let it be known that you must examine what you do. You must judge your own work to see if it measured up to your goal."

Wow! I can judge. I thought. *I can do what I've been warned not to do all my life.* My arm shot up. "Teacher, teacher, teacher!" I inquired. "How is it that I can judge when it is advised that I not?" Into my mind flashed the quote "Judge not —lest you be judged." No one wanted to be judged, so it was best not to judge, right?

Words can be tricky things. That is why on the other side we don't use them. Communicating by thought is much more effective. Thinking loses nothing in the translation the way words will. The telephone game doesn't work here.

In my mind flashed a history lesson. The lesson showed where we had been led off the path. A small error early on creates a big mistake. We learned not to judge because being judged by others is so damning. The intent of genesis isn't the same kind of damning judgment. Self-judgment is the kind of judgment that has been lost in our mistake of translation.

The difference here is only a word. That word can put us miles off course. In a world where words are required, we should be more conscious of the words we choose. Refusing to judge ourselves means we never look back and see where we went wrong. We blindly continue our course without making the necessary corrections to our actions.

Judgment was a harsh word. I feel more comfortable with the word *review*. Reviewing your life is an important step. I don't remember who said it, but "an unexamined life is not worth living."

Alton added in another perspective. We are to judge only ourselves and not others. Jumping into his thought stream, I see what he means. There is a big concern with people of earth being self-centered. The thought needs to be turned around. We need to be centered selves. When we are viable centered selves, then and only then can we contribute to the whole in a meaningful way.

Do you have many friends? Each is a little different. The same is true in spirit.

45

Homework

This was more than I could absorb in a single night. I had to take it home with me to work on. I was given a homework assignment and told to work on judging. I awoke the next morning, wondering how I was supposed to learn all this material. The parting words of the instructor faded away as I heard him say, "Start at the beginning. Take the first step."

The first step I took was to look at my world and myself. I

noticed something. I noticed how quickly I passed judgment on everything. I made a mental note to notice how many times a day I heard myself judging whether something was good or bad. I was surprised to learn how often I passed judgment. Coffee with cream was good. Coffee without cream was bad. My morning was starting out great. Was I going to keep this up all day?

I better hurry up, or I will be late for work, and that would be bad, I thought. The good driver who had never gotten a ticket got into her car and drove badly since she knew she was speeding again because she was late again. Bad. Bad. Bad.

This judgment stuff was wearing me out, and I had been awake only an hour. *I better get to the next step, or I will be too exhausted to learn.* I searched my mind and remembered what to do next. My teachers had said, "Judging is wrong, but reviewing is necessary."

I stopped judging and noticed I was noticing more things. I like cream in my coffee because it tastes better to me. Black coffee isn't bad. I just don't like black coffee. I won't even drink coffee if it is black. People who drink black coffee aren't bad. They aren't wrong because they have a different view than I do. I could accept the black coffee drinkers. Some of my best friends drink black coffee. My husband drinks black coffee.

Then, looking deeper and relaxed, I as a coffee drinker wasn't accepted either. There was the news report where they said coffee was bad. There it was again, that word *bad*. What was I to do now? Drink water? Did you hear the report on how bad some city water is? There I was again, stuck in the rhythm of heel toe, heel toe. I needed to take the next step.

I turned to my teachers. They quoted an earth saying. "Nothing is good or bad but thinking makes it so."

Great, I thought. I ask a question, and you quote Shakespeare. The common thoughts of the other side flooded my mind again. "We quote your Shakespeare to show you that earth has always had the answers."

I set out on working the steps. I can review but not judge. I use the review to guide my own life. I need to do the work of noticing things and deciding my path. If I don't judge ... then how do I make decisions? Many questions danced through my head. The stream was so relentless that my friends couldn't get a word in edgewise.

I was back to the same old dance. *Heel toe, heel toe, heel toe, I go.*

I knew I had to learn the next step. You can review your life and work, but when you are done, the only step you can end on is acceptance. I jumped ahead and questioned whether I accepted everything. Then how do I know what is good?

"Everything is good, my child" was the chorus that rang out from the other side. *Ah-ha*, I thought. I could accept that. I knew this to be true because when I died, I remembered the acceptance of all I had done in my life. Yes, I had gone off the path. Good thing I looked back to correct my steps.

Nothing is good or bad, right, or wrong, but thinking makes it so. What a revaluation! I was free of the need to judge. I could instead accept all steps as another step in the learning process. I was acceptable even if I was wrong. Others were acceptable even if they were wrong. The reason they were acceptable was because there is no right or wrong, only what is necessary to learn. I felt so much lighter. I felt so much better. Then the light broke through, allowing me to see more. I felt much love.

The next step of the near-death journey was illustrated to me. Once you review your life, you are accepted and loved. What a powerful feeling! I felt that I could love the world at this point. I realized I really did love the world at this point because I stopped judging. Could I keep this feeling when I returned to the real world of the earth?

What do you judge? What do you review? What do you accept? Development isn't easy.

46

Making More Room

When I stepped back and looked at myself, I had some concern that you, my readers, wouldn't understand. When I first came out of the closet, I decided that reality would have to make room for my semi-real world. Now I decided that you would have to make room for me too.

I have heard all there is about why I cannot experience the things that keep happening to me. I have yet to tell you my side, the inside story. I hear thoughts, not voices.

Another teacher stepped out to show me a story. He showed me a picture of a swollen belly, and I think a woman was about to give birth to a new thought. The picture panned backward, and I saw it was a picture of the swollen belly of a child who was starving. "Don't judge until you see the whole picture" was the lesson. (Many times, my friends show me things the way mediums see signs that mean something to them. It is like a game of charades.)

I reasoned my defense. Science claims we use only 10 percent of our brains. Maybe we are tapping into another 2 percent. The final answer isn't in yet. I don't claim to have all the answers. I only know there must be another answer.

Perhaps we must ask the right questions. This is one of the greatest side effects of learning from the other side. I have discovered that there is always another side.

What do you question? What do you so easily just accept? Once you question things, you think differently.

47

The ABCs of Time

Time on earth is different from time in the spirit. On the other side, it is more like times. It is not like there isn't a past; it's more like the past is now. There is also an expanded time that somehow reaches into possible futures. On the other side, they don't know about our time; they know only of timing, and timing is the stuff of synchronicity.

Linear time is something we are all accustomed to. We have lived it all our lives. We also know of nonlinear time. We just don't know we know of it. Nonlinear time is packed inside real time. It is as simple as the ABCs. Let me break it down for you.

Linear time is when everything is in order, such as A, B, C, and so forth. Real-time ABCs are how we manipulate these letters with such ease that we create language. When we were young, we learned to sing the ABCs. If we were stopped in midstream, we would need to start again from the very beginning to complete the task. Without our knowing it, we became so accustomed to the workings of the alphabet that we no longer had to recite the letters to use them. The wholeness of familiarity created a nonlinear alphabet, a more usable one. That is what nonlinear time is. Now do you remember?

This nonlinear thinking is the stuff of memories and future hopes. We can rescript our past and learn from our experiences to create a better future for others and ourselves. The "now" is the conjunction point, the intersection of nonlinear (spiritual) time and linear (material) time. In spiritual time we can jump from event to event. In material time we must wait for the ticking of the clock.

Knowing that linear (material) time and nonlinear (spiritual) time are so deeply embedded in each other and cannot be separated is as simple as understanding the ABCs. Spirit has been with us all the time. The problem is, we don't know how to recognize it.

Buckle up, readers. Things are going to get harder. Now I will test the real world.

PART 5

Confessions of a New Way

48

Synchronicities

The coincidences that seasoned my life were now becoming synchronicities. I was able to see another view of time. On the other side, they don't know about our time; they know only about timing, and timing is the stuff synchronicities are made of.

The coincidences were becoming more frequent and intense. They had progressed to the point of qualifying as synchronicities. I am a simple person. I don't feel comfortable with fancy terms. I just began to call them "Go figure." I was having quite a few "go figures" in my life.

Another story time here. I had to go out of town to help a person in trouble. It was a long drive, and we had to stop for the night. We went to a small store. They had outdated magazines: three in a pack for three dollars. We each chose a pack and settled in for the night.

I pulled my pack out and wanted the one on top. When I read the table of contents, there was an article about the very problem I was about to face. There was good advice in the article.

I was amazed and thanked my guides. Their answer surprised me. "Did you not know that we know what you need even before you do?"

Does good timing happen to you? I call it "Go figure." How could this possibly happen? Figure it out.

49

New Earth Friends

We had moved to a new house to get away from the harm that had been done to my daughter. Some of the people reading this next story might think the event is a coincidence. Some people will know better and see the hand of synchronicity at work. I think it is more, deeper, a "got to be." This was more than a "go figure." It was a "got to be." I must have planned some of this before I came to this life

I was making new friends as I went to school at night. I was also making new friends during the day. My new house gave me new neighbors. My new house and my new neighbor made me face two issues I had been running from all my life. The curious new neighbor introduced me to psychics and AA.

I had been born into an alcoholic family. I looked at my family but refused to see the problems. I wasn't the active addict. I was the active enabler. If my mother taught me anything, she taught me to be a good enabler. She and I stuck our heads in the ground and ignored what was happening. The only problem with this position is that you are leaving yourself wide open to be kicked in the butt.

The neighbor opened the door to learn about psychics. She talked openly about such things. We talked about many things. As friends do, we talked about troubles in our lives. The neighbor shared with me much information about the disease of alcoholism.

I remembered one of my teachers and the lesson of the limping man, and I knew this was another wake-up call. I wanted to learn from her. I tried to comfort her in her difficult life.

Periodically I was slapped in the face with issues that were trying to wake me up to what was around me. I would just slip further and further into sleep. There would come along a harder slap to awaken me to the issue. I would then start to come out of it and mumble something and then drift back into my comfortable sleep. You will be led again and again to the issues until you pay attention. I finally answered my wake-up call.

Now I was being shown another signpost that pointed to addressing addictions. That is why my soul decided on a life with an alcoholic father. That is why as an adult child I married an addict. The issue wouldn't go away.

I learned about the disease of alcoholism and the associated disorder of the enabler. The answer is nothing until you put it into action. I needed to learn more about addiction and AA.

My new neighbor was moving away. Before she left, she told me we would see each other again. She had seen herself sitting in an audience where I was a speaker. My nighttime friends had also spoken about such a thing. They said I wouldn't be listening to it until my hair was gray.

My eyes opened wide just before I rolled them again. I was only in my thirties at the time. Gray hair was a good thirty years away at least. I'm not a patient person. I was writing down all the lessons from my night journeys. This was note-taking like in school; it wasn't a book. I rolled my eyes and thought, *what do they know anyway?*

My coming out of the closet was very limited. I came out to my husband. Later, I found I liked writing with the help of Alton. My notes grew into a kind of journal but not a book. Not yet. I also found I could come out in my writings and still stay in the closet. The whole idea of confessions is that they are done after the fact as a way of releasing what you are holding inside. I write my imaginary book as a confessional. I write to you, my friends, of the future.

See how it works? The first thing I needed to do was work on myself.

50

Facing Myself

I said goodbye to my friend and wished her well. I was left alone again to deal with myself. It was easy to look at my friend and see how addiction was a problem. It was no longer easy to look at myself without seeing the same issue. The drug of choice wasn't alcohol. It was pot. The person was my husband. I wasn't the addict. I was the enabler.

I started to go to meetings. The AA meetings I started out at weren't very welcoming to me. CAPS (Children of Alcoholic Parents) was a group that helped me more. I bought books to supplement my learning about this issue. The books and meetings intensified my need to correct my life. I was waking up. I was starting to get it.

My husband and I had had many fights about this issue before. This time it was different because I was different. He said if I were nicer, he would quit. I was nicer, but he still didn't quit. He said he needed help, and if I were supportive, he would quit. I was supportive, but he didn't quit. He said I had let him get away with it, so why should he quit? I quit letting him get away with it, and he still didn't know why he should quit.

I was done with it. I had heard every lie and excuse in the book. Believe me when I tell you it is a very big book. But this time I was done with it. I didn't care what he did. I knew what I had to do. I turned to my closet.

I never really tried to be psychic before. Now I consciously focused on my husband. When he made a buy, I met him at the door and told him I knew what he had just done. I could keep track of him this way.

I called his friends and said they weren't to step into our house again if they supported my husband's lies and secrets. I called his mother and confessed that the money problems were because of the pot her son was on. My husband and I had a fight like we had never had before. We had a fight that finally worked.

He will have to tell the rest of that story. At the very first AA meeting he went to, he fully intended to leave; this thereby gave him time to smoke more pot before he came home. Something else happened. My husband has now been clean since April 1997. It is also a coincidence that he passed away on his clean date. He had been clean for twenty-two years.

I learned that I could work only on myself and not on others. Is it a common mistake you make too?

_____

_____

51

New Life

Now that I was done living my husband's life, I was more able to live my own. That is the funny thing about life. Life goes on. My world didn't come to a screeching halt because I no longer acted the way I did when I had been an enabler. It was as if I were waking from a dream, a very long and miserable one. The slap across the face of all the circling coincidences finally woke me up. That is how the spirit works. It keeps slapping you until you wake up, or you can continue to sleep. The choice is yours. The pain of the slap will eventually get so obvious that you will be stirred from your sleep.

Have you ever rejected a new way? When you are between a rock and a hard place, get out of the way so you don't get hit anymore.

52

Local School

I wanted to learn more about the psychic world. I signed up for a class the local school district offered. The class met once a week for a month, led by a bright and lively woman. She demonstrated the use of cards and encouraged us to explore numerology. A healer came to class to demonstrate the power within our hands and within our belief systems. The horoscopes were discussed. Hypnotism was demonstrated. A little bit of everything was touched on.

It was a banquet for this starving psychic. I tasted a bit of each area in the psychic field. I tasted what it was like not to be put down for being psychic. I appreciated her knowledge and support.

I compared these classes to what I was learning at my school in the sky. My teachers explained what was accomplished with each step the lively redheaded lady taught.

"There are many roads that lead to the same place," my teachers had said to start their lesson. "There are many methods of travel on the roads. Some may take a jet, such as the near-death experience. Others may choose the born-again experience available in many religions. Study of the occult will also lead you closer to your destination. Learning at the feet of a guru will get you well along the way."

There is one more thing here I must comment on. My teachers almost never put any method down. They wouldn't stoop to putting down anyone or anything. I thought it was just good manners in the beginning. Later, I learned that negative thinking is a trap that brings you down.

Do you judge and put things down? I learned to be discerning and allow each person his or her own path.

_____

_____

53

Readings

I have been able to read people all my life. I didn't know at the time that I was "reading." I knew only that at times the merging of thoughts happened. I have done enough readings to learn something about people. You can never read them completely.

A person is very much like a book. I can read a few pages of that book at times. I may read the section where the girl is spewing about how much she hates the young man with whom she just had a fight. I believe the young girl and the boy will break up. I never get to read the next chapter, where they make up and live happily ever after.

In the short two pages I read, I believed the boy was totally without redemption. I didn't get to read the previous chapter, in which the girl contributed to the deception. I have read enough people to know I didn't know the whole story.

My lively living instructor, who was teaching the class at the local high school, taught me another lesson, a very valuable one about readings. The instructor did private parties. She used her considerable talents to read for people who came. Each person would wait in another room and then come in and sit for a private reading. This party was in a very exclusive neighborhood.

Every woman who walked into the room was told she should learn more and start doing more for herself. The reader was putting her personal feelings ahead of the client's. Unless readers are disciplined and well trained, they will reveal as much about themselves as they will about the client.

I learned to be very careful about reading and readers. There is a big difference between reading and interpreting what you read. When my unworldly friends trained me, they taught me that this parlor game was no game. When we are very young, it is important that we have others read to us. Later, we must learn to read for ourselves so our education can continue. Most of all, my friends caution me that it is not only what you read that is important; it is what you read into it that is also important. Both must be watched closely.

Do you see the difference in readers? Reading is one thing. Telling you what to do is another.

54

New Church

I needed to be with people who would accept me for what I was. When I spoke about a chakra around my family, they thought I was swearing. I wanted to be able to ask about Kundalini without being asked whether that was some kind of food.

Later, when I introduce Ben, I will get into more of the Eastern path. Ben is another one of my spirit friends. I know most people call them spirit guides. They have been around for so long that I now consider them my friends. Ben is "a nickname. I cannot spell his real name. It's something like Benji, and that name just complicates my thoughts because all I see is that cute dog from the movie *Benji*. For now, let us get back to the story.

I found out about a religion that not only accepted what I was doing but also held classes about it. I started going to a spiritualist church. My mother said my grandmother would turn over in her grave if she knew I was going to another church. My mother thought I am going to hell because I was no longer Catholic. I told my mother, "If she is turning in her grave, she is turning to pay attention."

I met many wonderful people while I went there. One of them is still my friend. I'm not surprised that we stay in touch. I remember her from another life.

I remembered this day just like I was remembering something that happened last week. This day I was remembering was the last day of that life. It was strange to see myself, or the person I knew I had been then, having a great old time in a pub in England.

My best friend and I were getting ready to leave together. We walked toward the door, and I noticed two men watching us. I was worried about them and started heading back inside. These men pushed us outside, and the next thing I knew my screaming had stopped. I realized my throat had been cut, and now the sound was cut short because of it. I reached up to my throat and was surprised by how hot the blood was. There was steam rising from the wound as I died.

As I stood there, watching my body, I realized I had contributed to my death by drinking. I vowed not to ruin my life by drinking again. The synchronicities of my life were setting me up once again. I had ignored my prior invitations to address the addiction problems in my life.

Later, I will get into remembering past lives. The important thing to notice here is that I chose a life that would instill in me a desire *not* to drink. The story of addictions was important to learn here. Later in life, it would hover around me yet again as I faced another difficult matter.

Do you remember a life gone by? Remember the lesson of the life, not the way he or she died. That is the whole point of lives gone by.

55

The Dark Lady

I still wanted to see human teachers. I joined a meditation group at the local spiritualist church. I made a few friends there and enjoyed the services as much as I did the studies. Then a new woman rejoined the group. We really ruffled each other's feathers. This woman had been a member in years past and had just resurfaced.

She insisted that the room be totally dark during meditation class so we could contact the spirit guides who would help us. She had been in the business for some time. She knew everything. Her strict rules must be followed to the letter. I insisted on separating the method from the meat the way my friends had taught me. "We meditated just fine up to now without those black curtains," I pointed out.

I was in trouble once again. I swear one of the lessons I will never learn is when to keep my mouth shut. It's not that I reject all authority; I just reject empty-headed authority. She looked at me with eyes that could kill. You don't have to be psychic to know how she felt about me.

The rest of the class progressed as it had before her arrival. We started every meeting with a prayer for protection. We then sang a spiritual song to raise the energy level. Then came the best part, the quiet time where we would go within. I thought I was behaving. I sat there quietly and waited to see what would happen. She called an end to the meditation. We were each asked to relate what we had experienced while we were in meditation.

We went around in a circle and related each story. I related my experience. My uncle was undergoing heart surgery the next day, so my thoughts, prayers, and meditations were on him. Into me flooded a picture of my uncle standing in front of me in perfect health. Through a little pinprick in the middle of his chest, a light was shining through.

I questioned whether the hole meant trouble in his heart would lead to problems during the upcoming surgery. The picture in my mind reacted to my question by sucking me into the light on the other side of his heart. There I was again, bathed in the light. I understood that whatever happened the next day didn't matter because my uncle had the light in his heart.

The dark curtain lady conducting the meeting assured me that I was totally wrong. She didn't mask her feelings toward me. "You should not meditate on personal things. You should not share such things with the rest of the group," I was crisply told. "We are here to contact our spirit guides and read the other people at the meeting the way I am doing."

Her instructions to the group as we started every night were to leave whatever we personally felt at the door. The next meeting began with her storming out of the room because I was there. She objected to my being there because I didn't think the way she thought. She wouldn't tolerate otherwise.

She said I was doing everything wrong and messing up her group. I still don't totally understand this. I know what it is like because I saw myself in her. I often wanted things my way. I know I was threatening her reality, and she was acting defensively. I felt we were very much alike yet so very different.

Can you see why I am in the closet? Even among the like-minded, I am in trouble.

56

Seeing Ourselves

I see. I see. I see the lady inside me. On earth we are bound to meet people who are just like us. We also run into people who aren't like us. When we don't like the person we are looking at, we need to look inside ourselves and find out why. I am here to tell you I didn't like the dark lady. She was very wicked to me.

My friend and adversary at the meditation group couldn't accept me. I must be doing something wrong if I don't agree with her. Was I looking at some strange kind of mirror where I saw me, but there was someone else standing there? I saw how wrong I could be when I thought I was right. I didn't know I was wrong until I learned another way of looking at things.

This is the biggest advantage of working with my unseen friends. I was learning to look at things differently. I could see through their eyes and know their truths, even if they were different than mine. Reality seems less real when you realize reality is constructed by what you believe to be real, not what is real.

How can opposing realities both be real? I questioned my friends and myself. "If birds of a feather flock together … why do opposites attract?" That is a question I put to them and to myself. "How can contradictions be true?" Now they were obliging my inquiry by illustrating the next lesson.

When I was young, I learned to be like everyone else. I was the poster child for my family's beliefs. I didn't step out of the mold until I went to college and learned not everyone thought like my family did. What a shock to me!

Up to that point in my life, I thought "One" was my nickname because many people referred to me as "One of those [insert family name here] kids." I had no separate identity or thoughts. It never occurred to me that there might be another way to look at things. My mother often said to me, "If I tell you the sky is green and the grass is blue, then that is the way it is." There was no questioning the way things were.

My friends, my wonderful unseen friends, were teaching me differently. They were the opposite of everything my mother taught. They were the opposite of everything the world taught. I learned by being attracted to the opposite. That is why we are here on earth. They had worked in another answer to my questions.

Everyone has his or her own idea of what heaven is like. I can tell you what heaven is like for me. I remember when I had my near-death experience. That is about as close as you can get to heaven and still come back.

Heaven is where you belong. That is the whole reason heaven is so great. Everyone there is just like you. You are all birds of a feather that flock together. On the other side, you will reside exactly where you belong; be it heaven or hell, you will find yourself right at home there.

Let me make one thing perfectly clear. I know there is no hell. There is a place I wouldn't like to be. I will call that place "hell." I will call the placement of you with others like yourself "heaven." We don't all belong in the same place when we go to the other side. Thank God, I would hate to be stuck in someone else's idea of heaven because for me that would be hell. (The Joker thinks this is wonderfully witty.)

Whatever section of heaven you are in, I will guarantee you only one thing. You are never alone. God will always be close to you. If this weren't true, it wouldn't be heaven. In heaven you meet only what makes you happy, not what makes you grow. There is only one thing that will interrupt your heaven. Others will visit you from other districts, spheres, sections, and realities.

Birds of a feather do attract. Opposites attract. You will notice an attraction to others that aren't like you. You will notice something outside your heaven. You will remember a part of yourself that was human. You will remember parts of yourself that are yet to become. The difference will help you, just as on earth. You will have the opportunity to adjust your outlook on things. Heaven is very much like earth.

"You cannot grow and change if all remains the same," Alton reminds me. "After a period of rest and study, you will again feel the urge to grow." We may have been thrown out of paradise in the Bible. I see it as more of a choice. We chose to partake of the tree of knowledge. Paradise shrank and was no longer capable of making you completely happy.

We try to create heaven on earth by insisting that everyone be just like us. We want to rule the world. We want everyone to be the same religion. We want exactly what we want. This would be heaven. But I have learned that heaven isn't all it's cracked up to be, because we also need earth. We need the part that isn't like us.

All for now.

All for now? Many lessons are ended like this. There is more to come.

57

Another Answer

One month later, the lady with the black curtains was still shooting daggers at me every time she saw me. She was holding onto the belief that to become spiritual, we must follow certain exact steps. My friends had taught me differently. I was defending my own beliefs too. How can we resolve a war if I cannot resolve the chasm between the dark lady and me?

I once again turned to my closet. I opened the door that would lead to the school in the sky. I sat down. I asked my mentor and friend to help me see about the dark lady and me. I noticed something else as I sat there. My questions were becoming different. I no longer badgered the spirits with demands to know whom I could hate for hurting my daughter. I felt a need to learn to understand me, understand others, and understand them.

I didn't help my husband get over his addiction. I helped myself get over needing to help him. I was beginning to learn that I couldn't help my daughter unless I helped myself. If my daughter was to get better, I would have to show her the way. But first, I had to learn the way myself.

"Dear, dear little one, it is indeed a joy and a job to answer all your questions." Class had begun. "We will assist you in your inquiry to understand why people don't get along.

"You ask why you cannot seem to become friends. You still believe that friends are the only good things to be. Look into yourself and see the lady. She is as determined to be right as much as you are. She reflects yourself.

"You are well accustomed to the colors that are about people as they go about their thoughts." The teacher was referring to my ability to see auras. "You have seen the colors change as quickly as a person can change their mind. You will now learn what those changing colors can mean.

"This is the perfect opportunity to teach you how you are like colors. As you sit before us, we see you as very intense colors. Your excitable and accessible colors make it possible for us to communicate. The hard part is for you to learn to control your colors and conditions. The red of your anger is just as vibrant as the pink of your love. We ask you, dear little one, to clear your screen so the lesson can begin.

"People are like colors. The colors of the rainbow can make your heart sing. Each color knows its place as they separate and combine to create beauty. Every color is beauty. Don't judge the value of the colors. Accept that each color has a place and a purpose as they combine and separate to create the reality in which you live. Together the colors create something that is almost real. A rainbow is real yet somehow unreachable and delicate. A rainbow isn't real; it is an effect. You are creating the effect of the world. You are creating the colors that paint the hue of the world you live in.

"Know you, my child, that you are like these colors. You and your feelings create the colors that you are. You know yourself well enough to recognize when you are red hot such as you were when you first came to class today. You also can feel now the cool blue of your being as you sit and listen to the lesson. So, now that you know you are colors, you can answer your own question of why people don't get along. Some colors clash, and some colors harmonize.

"Look now to yourself and be the soft blue you are feeling. Look now to the one you are struggling with and be her bright orange. Feel now the conflict between the blue and the orange colors. These colors don't seem to get along. Remember now the red anger you were when you were with her. The red and the orange do harmonize. You are what you need to be.

"Don't judge the value of the colors. Accept that all colors have a place and a purpose. All for now."

Did you think colors were only for the chakras? Colors have more uses, here and in healing.

58

Good Morning

The real world starts with the sound of the alarm going off. I knew I had better complete my notes before I forgot too much of the lesson.

What do they mean by "see that lady in me"? I thought as I recorded the lesson of the colors. I just wanted to know how to become friends, and they said to accept that we weren't. *I see. I see.* I do see her in me. They are right. I don't like how she acts toward me. I see this is how I appear to others.

Coming out of the closet has created many situations where I don't belong. When I first started stating my case, I was very defensive about my position. This appeared as offensive to many other people. I was fighting a little too hard to claim my little piece of the world.

The nuns saw me as evil—not because I was truly evil but because my beliefs were so different from theirs. I feel like a weather front moving in. When two distinct weather patterns push on each other, there will be a storm. I know two things now. One, the weather will change. Two, the world will always be in a state of changing.

When I was still a very little girl, I asked my Old Man Friend why we must have such cold winters. Living in Michigan, I see the extremes of both summer and winter. I asked why God couldn't make everything even out and stay at a certain temperature all the time.

My Old Man Friend explained that the differences were necessary to keep the planet going. "Even as there is a need for the seasons, there is a need for the tropics and the polar caps," he explained. I had never thought of that before. "There is a need because there is a reason for the differences," he continued. In my mind flashed pictures of the sun and the tilt of the earth and how and why things are. I understood it better. I still thought God could do it if he wanted to.

Now, as I look back, I see how this lesson applies. The perfect sameness belongs in the perfect heaven. On earth we don't have the perfect balance. My Leader reminds me that we do have the perfect imbalance.

As night finally came and I lay me down to sleep, I knew the rest of the lesson wouldn't keep.

"The important lesson to learn from colors is that you are in control of your colors." They had begun their lesson. I was always amazed at how they could just pick up on a lesson as if no time had passed. I wondered whether they even knew time had passed. I wondered whether time had really passed.

"Don't judge the goodness of the colors. Every color will serve its purpose. You will change your colors as you go about your day. God resides in the orange as much as he does in the blue. The red orange of flames will bring about change. Blue cannot bring change.

"You are indeed lucky that you can change your color. Think now about what that means. You are not only the created but also the creator. Even further, my child, you aren't only the creator. You can observe, analyze, adapt, and then create. Creation has a pattern to it. You are in control of that pattern. We do forget at times that we have this ability within us. We change as we go about our day with intent and purpose. We go along with the flow without realizing we create that flow.

"You are colors, my child, many, many wonderful colors. Another lesson you must learn is what you are doing with your colors. When you go off the path, it is not because you don't care. It is because you are unaware. Now, my child, class for this day is finished. Go about your work this day and become aware of your colors and what you are creating with them. The colors you choose will make it a joy or a job. Go, my little one. All for now."

There it was the answer to another one of my questions. I started my notetaking when I woke up. There are many steps to learn.

1. The colors are the effect of our thoughts.
2. Our thoughts are creating the circumstances in which we live.
3. We are in control of our thoughts.
4. Changing the way we think can change the hue of the world.

I wondered whether I could put this information to practical use in my life. I knew I wanted to be able to control my life. I had forgotten that it started with controlling myself.

I still feel uncomfortable with the dark lady. I am aware of how she hurts me. She is only aware that I'm not what she likes. We are both unaware of a better way. The dark lady at church taught me that I couldn't change others. My friends taught me to change only myself. I think we all have more to learn. "Heaven help us" is both a plea and a prayer.

Does it make more sense now? That is why they said, "All for now," leaving us time to think about it.

59

Defending Heaven

We aren't in heaven. We are on earth, where things aren't always the way we want them to be. My friend and adversary at the meditation group couldn't accept me. I must be doing something wrong if I didn't agree with her. My spirit friends teach me that all things are acceptable, even those things we don't want to accept.

We sometimes need someone to show us what we are like when we are wrong. When we don't like what we see in others, then we need to change that very thing about ourselves. I did more than see that lady in me. I saw me in that dark lady.

There was a great conflict between the dark lady and me. There was a mini war. This is the part of me I recognized in the dark woman. I tend to fight when I know I am right or at least when I feel I am right because I cannot accept another way. My spirit friends tell me I had to meet this woman so I could meet myself.

I was admitting to my warring ways with the dark lady when I was smack-dab in the middle of another war with my friends. When you begin a spiritual search, you are advised to go within to find your answers. No one tells you what to do when what you find is in direct conflict with what you believe.

I am thin skinned and thickheaded, and getting through to me isn't an easy task. It is a good thing that my spirit friends didn't give up on me. There was a lesson to which I had much resistance. I had already accepted and learned so much from them, but this was different. This was *un*acceptable. This was impossible. This shattered even my conception of reality.

The lesson they wanted to teach about was in direct conflict with everything I held to be true. The lessons made me question all I had been taught to believe in. The lesson cut so deep that it made me question everything I had been taught not to believe in. How could I give up heaven when the only alternative I knew was hell? Reincarnation? I couldn't buy into the great record keeper in the sky, who demanded payment for everything ever done. I didn't experience this in the God I knew when I died. What happened when I died?

People have spoken about what happened when they died. Books and scientists are even beginning to talk about what happens when people die. But religions don't talk about it. At least my religion didn't speak of such things.

My school in the sky had all the wonderful lessons I find echoed in different religions throughout the world. What about that? Where does that fit in? There are a few religions that accept such things. Most religions have an esoteric side that sounds very much like some of the things I am going through. See what confusion a little research can bring.

I knew what the subject matter was that the leader wanted me to learn about. I knew it was relevant and necessary to continue in my studies. I also knew I would have nothing to do with it. I was handling the situation the way I usually handled things I didn't like. I ignored it. Their familiar call of "Time for a lesson, my child" was answered by a quick "Go away. I'm busy." I'm not an easy student. The only thing harder to break than a bad habit is a closed mind. I was a tough nut to crack.

I wouldn't budge until I saw the dark lady in me. I didn't know what I would be when I changed my ways, but at least I knew I wouldn't be like that dark lady. Being unable to change is making me unable to grow. That wasn't something I wanted. I decided to go to class and at least listen. I went to class. I was in a very, very bad mood.

Have you ever needed to change? Yet changing is scary.

60

This Means War

I knew the subject matter of today's lesson would be about the continuation of life. I would have nothing to do with any of it. I couldn't stand it if my concept of heaven was destroyed. On the upside, though, this also meant my concept of hell would be nullified. I didn't know much about reincarnation. All I knew for sure was that I didn't agree with it. What about the belief that there is nothing when you are dead? I knew that wasn't true from personal experience. Now what?

I had sat in on many of the Leader's lectures by this time. The awe and fear I had felt for him in the beginning had worn off.

My Leader stood in front of a packed house. Alton, the Joker, George, and others were there by my request to give me support. There were about twenty other beings there. Most of them I didn't know.

When the Leader quieted the class and started the lesson, I tried to listen. I tried. I tried. I really tried, but I failed. I was immediately on what I call "the defensive" and others would call "an attack." It would depend on which side of my anger you were on. "But, dear leader, how can that be?" I asked him accusingly.

The golden Leader gently advised me to use my inner eyes to

see to the depths of what I wished to study. Slowly but surely, I would come to see how things worked when I learned more about the subject. I hadn't yet taken Patience 101, so I didn't want to wait.

I could stand it no more. I stood right up, planted both feet firmly on the ground, put my hands on my hips, looked him straight in the eyes, and said, "Prove it." This isn't exactly the wisest thing to do with a spirit as mighty as the Leader. I had seen his response to students who had gotten out of line before. I had in fact been that student before but had never dared to go this far before. There I stood, looking at him, wishing I hadn't stood up and being grateful that I had.

The Joker said, "Look out. She is starting to spark." In the spirit world, you throw out sparks when you are angry. Thankfully, the Leader was used to me by this time. He called me "his little spirit with entirely too much spirit for her own good." He looked back at me and started laughing. That did it. I was getting very upset. I was mad. I was irate. I really started to burn.

The Joker made great fun of taking out an army helmet and putting it on his head. The other classmates ran for whatever cover they could find. Even the ever-proper Alton materialized a Roman shield and hid behind it. "Look out. She is really burning now!" everyone was shouting with great glee.

The Leader by this time had totally lost control of the class and himself. He stood in front of us, laughing so hard tears were coming from his eyes. He managed to ask, "Must I use this water to put out your great fire?"

I understood then what I needed to learn. I also understood what the lesson of the dark lady was. She wouldn't hear anything different than what she believed. I knew she was wrong for not listening. I knew I was wrong for not listening. I was wrong to fight about it. I realized my error and sat down to listen to the lesson. At the end of the lesson, the Leader pulled me aside and said, "You are being allowed to have a special teacher. When Bendiji is finished with you, you may return to class." Bendiji was to be my private tutor. I was being sent to remedial discipline class. Who am I kidding? I was being sent to detention again.

Have you been to detention? It sometimes takes a whole lot to admit you were wrong.

61

The Continuation of Life

If you wish to learn about the continuation of life, you must look to the plants. Do you see the bloom, my child? You are like the flower. You can watch it grow from a speck, live in glory in the sun, then shrivel and fade and be no more.

This would be true if you considered that lifetime to be all there is to that flower. The speck it grew from is of seasons past, and when the flower's time is over, it will leave yet another piece of itself to yet bloom again. I ask you, my child, "Are you the flower that blooms this season or the next, and did you not get your start in seasons past?"

This is the first obstacle you must overcome if you are to understand how life goes on. There is a part of you that existed in different times. You may not recognize your starting point. What you leave behind you to yet carry on isn't what you can see. But you are more than you can see.

During this life as a flower, you knew that as you fed from the sun, you were also drinking from the earth. This is the duality of spirit and matter. You also knew there were others than thee. There is life outside of me.

My child, you are this flower. I ask you to look around. Do you see the flowers that are next to you? There are many more around just like you. Look further, my child, and you will see that you aren't just a flower; you are also part of a bush.

As a part of a bush, you can see that you still grow, bloom, and fade; but you know that you are more than just a flower. You know you aren't alone. You are connected to the bush. You aren't the whole bush, yet you are the bush. It's the same with you, my child, and your connection to the all.

Another obstacle to understanding the continuation of life is that life continues through others. The ends of your being are only where you draw the line. The connection, the continuation, the extension continues. Remember, little one, you are never alone.

Look around you more, my little flower. You will see there are others around who are not like you. Some don't have your beauty. Some don't have your scent. Some are bigger. Some are smaller. Some of what you observe aren't even flowers. They don't appear to be like you. They are subject to the same conditions of growth and life. They are more like you than they first appear. Can you, my flower, know you extend beyond the bush into the meadow that surrounds you?

When you look at yourself, my lovely little flower, do you not also see that your beauty and scent attract a bee? Do you not now see that your purpose is not only to be but also to give to other too? When you start to look around you more, you will see more and more than you knew before.

You, in your beauty of the flower, look down and don't see the importance of the grass. It has neither your beauty nor your scent. What can it possibly contribute? Do you find yourself wondering why the cow passes you up and instead is attracted to the grass that is more to the cow's liking? Do you think the cow is foolish and the bee wise?

There is another obstacle that blocks your growth. There is learning you cannot know. There is knowing what you have yet to know. All the accumulated knowledge is but a beginning and a foundation for what will become you.

Now, once again, dear child, when you look around you more, you will see more wisdom than you could see before. My child, will you look some more?

My wonderful little flower, is it not wonderful that you can see your place and purpose? Isn't it even better that you can understand how others not like you can have a place and purpose too? You can rest, knowing your place and being at peace with the others around you. Can you, my child? I now ask you to contemplate the bee and the cow and all that is beyond them too.

Once again, I ask of you more, to look around for more to know. All for now.

There they go again. This lesson will be applied later as we think about it.

PART 6

Confessions from the East

62

Bendiji

Working with my new teacher, my detention overseer, would help me in ways I could never have anticipated. My discipline teacher was to instruct me in the ways of the Eastern religions. I didn't even know I lacked discipline. The first lesson, the most important one I was taught, was the very first step you should take before you start on any spiritual practice. Before you get to know anything else, get to know yourself.

Now, another layer was being added to me. An Eastern-thought layer. I am once again getting ahead of myself here by showing how an understanding of Eastern thought gave yet another facet to the jewel of my being. I was learning to apply the lesson that had been given to me by my unseen friends. The story of the crystal has a practical application. I was beginning to understand that the more facets and details a jewel has, the more it is worth. I was no longer a diamond in the rough. I was beginning to take form. Bendiji (Ben), my discipline teacher, would add another facet to my training and me.

Are you ready for more to know?

_____

_____

63

Mysterious Easterners

Many people lack an understanding of psychic or spiritual work, because it is so foreign to their nature. As a born and bred Westerner, there is nothing harder to understand than the mysterious East. That is one of the reasons I was being sent to Ben. I needed to complete myself, and there was this gaping hole in me that comprised the missing pieces of the Eastern gifts. I needed to learn about the other side. I thought the other side was the psychic side, and then I thought the other side was the spiritual side. Now I find there is another side. It is the Eastern side. There are many sides to us.

There is a picture in my head once again of the Chinese handcuffs. This little paper toy has tied up many of us. There was a lesson to be learned and wisdom to be acquired. If we stop using force and work to understand it, we will be free of what traps us. There is so much to learn from Ben and his Eastern ways that it's necessary to devote a whole section of this book to him. In the end, I spent more time with Ben than with the Leader. I needed to learn so much.

Sometimes the thing most foreign to us can teach us the most.

64

First Impressions

I remember our first meeting. He extended his arm to invite me to sit under his tree with him. He was so warm and gentle that I couldn't resist his invitation. He was like no spirit I had met before. George felt like peace. Ben was something beyond peace. He somehow encompassed a nothingness that had substance. I think it was his training that extinguished his ego. This lack of ego was so enticing. It felt like a big, black hole pulling me in, and I couldn't wait to see what he would teach me.

George was peace. George had taught me to be at peace with myself, but Ben would teach me to be at peace with others. He was a man of few words. Alton was a word wizard. His short sentences were often quotable quotes, but Ben was Eastern; he was different. I will never forget what he said to me the first time we met. When he raised his arm to invite me to join him under the tree, he said, "Sit." We sat ... and sat ... and sat.

Do you also need to slow down and just sit?

_____

_____

65

On Second Thought

My meetings with my new guide went a little better as time went on. He spoke more. We didn't just sit. He asked what I thought. Thought? Thought about what? I didn't know what to tell him. I didn't want to just blurt something out. I felt like this was a trap. I started to think about what to say.

"Good. Very good" was his reply. "I can see you are starting to think more and talk less." This lesson was about Confucius. I had heard of him. Others said he was just confusing because he thought about things differently than those around him. Just like with the dark lady, I could see a little of me in him. This was going to be interesting.

Thinking was the lesson of the day. It doesn't matter what you think; it does matter *that* you think. He taught me how to examine things, to look and think instead of just going along or rebelling. These were the two methods I was very used to.

He showed me how to use the pearls. In spirit you think in pictures, much the way my leader showed me the wallet full of pictures to show what he was. Ben showed me a string of pearls. Each pearl was a thought stream, where everything followed in line. Examining the pearls would show me where the idea we were thinking about had its root and where we would end up if we followed it. I could better see the flaws in the thought streams because the pearls would become less pure and full of different colors, like they were being infected by a misconception and turning from white to a different hue.

It is now like we cannot wait for the next lesson. Will you join me?

66

Going Out East

I started to read books about Eastern thoughts. I learned *chakra* isn't a swear word. Chakra is a part of your body that receives and deploys energy. I learned *Kundalini* isn't Italian food. Kundalini is when the chakras within you begin to work together. Meditation isn't an attempt to leave your troubles behind. Meditation is the gateway to the spiritual process.

When I was growing up, meditation was never discussed. Prayer was the only thing the faith of my family endorsed. I have prayed all my life. Prayer is something I am comfortable with. Meditation was new to me. I learned meditation is more than just sitting funny and chanting. The way I have come to understand the difference between the two disciplines is prayer; it is talking to God. Meditation is listening to God.

I was taught to believe that meditation was an oddity of an odd religion. All other religions were looked upon as suspect. Suspect of what, I was never sure of. I was warned never to indulge myself with looking into them.

I can understand why those in most religions distance themselves from other beliefs. I wonder whether those in the religions understand what they are doing when they act this way. I compare the way I was brought up to living in the dark ages. Everything around me was evil and bad. Only I, or those who thought like me, was good. If they (anyone who doesn't think like I do) don't submit to my beliefs, I will launch a crusade against them.

I wonder whether the faith of my family understands that I wasn't led away from my founding religion by some strange other religion, I was pushed away by an inadequate religion. In the end, I had to turn away from my religion of origin. My faith is another matter. The groundwork of my faith is still strong. My faith is of God, of the all, of the source. Learning about the faith of others has enhanced my faith.

I found solace in the famous poem "A Road Less Traveled." My destiny led me to a fork in the road. My free will allowed me to walk in whatever direction I chose. I could resume my old upstanding way of life and not be scorned by my family. I could turn to my Old Man Friend again. I could find out what lay beyond my predefined boundaries. I could take another path. The crossroads of deciding to find my own way were what caused the turbulence leading to my little fiasco in class. My life is a road less traveled. Now I was being challenged to accept the path with my conscious mind. I was using my free will to do the right thing.

I decided long ago that the world had to make room for my psychic beliefs. The world also had to learn to accept my spiritual friends. Now I was asking myself to make room for Eastern beliefs. Jumping ahead to the end of the lesson, I now know what I was doing. I was making myself whole. The missing part of me was being reintroduced to me.

Let me see if I can make this clear. The Western world condemns destiny because we believe in individual freedoms. The Eastern world condemns the individual as an ego that must be overcome. I objectively watch the West and the East. I subjectively feel the East and the West.

Are you still with me? Have you started a new path for yourself?

67

Guided to the Park

The easiest meditation is a guided meditation. I was going to give this meditation stuff a shot. I would try, but I wouldn't conform. It just wasn't in my nature.

There is a facilitator for this meditation. This person will lead you in a relaxation technique that usually requires you to breathe. I had to breathe anyway, so I figured it wouldn't hurt. I planted both feet on the ground the way I was instructed. I was used to planting both feet on the ground whenever I was determined to keep things my way. This too I was willing to cooperate with. I put my hands on my lap, facing upward, because apparently this was also important. I closed my eyes and waited for this meditation stuff to start working.

A guided meditation leads you down a rosier path. The facilitator asked each of us in the group to picture a path in our minds that led down into a beautiful meadow. We were then instructed to imagine trees, streams, flowers, or anything that was all cutesy. This was where the facilitator lost me.

I wasn't about to cooperate anymore. I had never been a person who could be easily led. This lady wouldn't lead me astray. This was as far as I would willingly go. The rebel in me decided I would create something I could never have. I live in the middle of a big city, so I could never find isolation. I have seen plenty of beautiful landscapes. I have never been to a desert, and dry land just doesn't exist where I live. I envisioned a dry land where the only decorations were the upcropping of rocks I rested on as I watched the sun in the distance.

When the meditation was over, the facilitator brought us back from our travels; I did feel very relaxed. I liked this meditation and thought it was worthwhile. I thought nothing more of it until the following week. I had taken my children to the zoo. I was relieved to see all the natural beauty around me. The zoo was like a park with many trees and grass.

When my children and I came to a play area, the kids asked me to stop. The play area was full of sand, toys, and rocks for the children to climb on. There in the middle was the exact rock I had pictured in my meditation. I sat on the rock and knew there was more to this meditation stuff than was apparent. My unseen friends gathered around and sat with me as I watched the sun go down. I knew I would return here again and again in my future meditations. I knew I had to learn more about meditating.

I no longer ask for support. I sense we are now fellow travelers.

68

More Meditations

There are many methods of meditation. Daydreaming is one method of meditation that comes naturally to most people. Watching a fire is my favorite way to meditate. My friends want me to insert that meditation is also contemplation. The common factor is that while you are meditating, you aren't thinking. You aren't planning what you are thinking; you are only gone. You don't even realize you are gone until you suddenly return. If you were planning, you would be using your left or active mind. Meditation, as the Easterner teaches, shuts down the left or active mind. The Western way of meditation is to trick the left mind into taking the back seat. It's easier for me to trick the left mind than to silence this active thinker.

It's while you are contemplating something that there is a lull in the thought stream, that little gap where you enter the timelessness of spirit. At first, you won't even notice it. Eventually, that little gap will get bigger. You will notice it only because you realize you are back. Back from where? It doesn't matter. Just breathe again.

You cannot make "it" happen. It just happens. How did it work for you?

69

Discovering Meditations

I discovered that meditating isn't what they say it is. I couldn't sit in the position the Eastern experts recommend. I did what was comfortable for me. Maybe I was doing it wrong. It started working for me. The Easterners say that when you meditate, you are seeking Nirvana, which means a state of nothingness. You notice things you never noticed before. You think things you never thought before. You stop your internal dialogue long enough to allow your other side to start talking too.

Meditating is an ongoing relationship between yourself and

God. Meditating supports the spiritual side of you. I'm not very good at remaining quiet and listening. Ben is a very good coach.

I tried out this meditation stuff. I didn't think I would be very good at it. The impossible did happen. I remained quiet for more than five minutes. I was still a hyperactive suburban entity who packs too much into her life. Now I was learning to be still. I never thought I could enjoy just sitting still and doing nothing. While you meditate, you don't *do* anything. You don't move. You don't do. I knew this was something I wouldn't be very good at. But I was trying.

Don't try. Do or do not. LOL Star Wars and the Eastern Jedi.

70

Mustang Meditation

I tried out this meditation stuff and worked on cleaning up my chakras. It's not that they were dirty; they needed to be cleaned up because they were rusty from disuse. I began to compare my chakra system to the old Mustang my husband was trying to restore.

He worked on each individual part of the engine. The cooling system, the combustion system, the braking system—there were a lot of separate systems that needed to work together to start the engine and make driving safe.

I started working on each of the seven major chakras. I learned where each of them was. I learned what each of them does. All cars come with an owner's manual. The Eastern books on the subtle energy system were like my new owner's manual.

I tried to do what the books instructed. The chakras are said to be like wheels that spin once you get them going. Mine were stuck. I tried working on them for months to get them started. I shined them. I greased them. I tried moving them with my mind's hands. Now and then, there was a slight rumbling from the engine that encouraged me.

Then it happened, just like the books said. I felt the wheels start to move. It started at the bottom and slowly moved up my body. I was an observer, noticing how each cell of my body grew in energy I was sure would break out of my skin. Just when I thought I could stand it no more, it shot out of my head. I breathed a sigh of relief and was glad it was gone.

It was a week before I had the nerve to do any more meditating. If I did it once, I could do it again, I reasoned. I made a conscious effort to start my engine again. *Grind. Grind. Grind.* Nothing was happening. I must be doing something wrong. I once again started paying attention to each chakra to understand what each part of me had to say. I wanted to feel it rise within me once again.

I was coaxing myself to make the energy rise within me when I noticed a strange thing. The energy in my head was making me feel like my brain was on fire. The chakra at the top of my head had started spinning while I was concentrating on my root chakra. I observed the movement of the energy as it once again traveled across my body. I was worried because I had it backward. I was supposed to be raising myself toward better things, and the energy was headed downward. What was I to do now? This wasn't expected. As suddenly as it had started, it ended with a tingling that remained for some time.

As I came out of my meditation, Ben stood in front of me. He was looking at me with disbelief. I thought I was really in trouble. He was going to tell me that I had destroyed my chakra system like blowing the engine I had worked so hard to restore.

"My little one, my little one," Ben greeted me. "You have done nothing wrong. All energy must complete a circuit. Your mission is not only to rise but also to utilize the energy and bring it down. You have done well, even if it is not what you expected."

Spirit is full of the unexpected. Have you been pleasantly surprised yet?

71

My Straight Job

I couldn't work a normal job during this difficult period of my life. I could no longer leave my children with a babysitter. I had to find a way to work on my own terms. Delivering newspapers early in the morning before anyone else woke up worked fine for me. I loved it.

My friends often accompanied me on my route and talked and taught as we went. I walked for miles and then suddenly notice I was done. I didn't know it then, but I was in a meditative state as I walked.

Some of you reading this book may wonder how to do meditation. Others reading this book have been meditating for some time. There are even those among you who meditate and don't realize they are doing it, just as I have done in the mornings. Meditation is easier than you think.

Boundaries were broken even in the morning. As I walked in the early morning, there was nothing alive around but me and the trees. I noticed that the trees would talk to each other in the quiet of the mornings. I noticed different personalities in the different types of trees. The pines that don't slumber during the winter keep the knowledge of years gone by. The trees that lose their dressing every year awaken and know their place is to grow anew each time. A little bigger, a little wider, a little stronger. A little better each year.

Early in the morning, there was nothing to distract me. It was only my friends, my nature, and me. Meditation is a singular project. Best when done alone. I watched the sun come up. I watched the seasons change. I began to watch me change.

I am forever grateful to my teachers and friends. I find it hard to separate them at times. A single instructor teaches some lessons. Other lessons are taught in unison. "When one becomes all," Alton explains. Then they would start. It was time for another lesson.

I share the lessons now and not just my experiences. Have you seen the difference?

72

Loving My Job

I watched the sun come up. I watched the seasons change. I enjoyed the experience and the freedom. I could never meditate while sitting there with my legs crossed. My body cannot bend that way. That is why I thought I must be doing something wrong. I learned I couldn't be doing it wrong if I was getting it right.

While I walked, I mulled over what I had learned in class. The current teachers were my ladies. The auric field that emanated from them was a soft pink and lavender. They were so close and operated so in tune with each other that they seemed to be one being. The two ladies taught in the gentlest of ways. "Excuse me please," they would say. "There is something that you must know. We thought you might like to hear this." Their gentleness was in direct conflict with their immense knowledge. When they greeted me, I always perked up and paid great attention. I knew I was in for a treat when they taught a lesson.

"A green thumb is one of God's greatest gifts. To be able to nurture a living plant and to in turn be nurtured by the plant illustrate how important it is to learn to give and receive." My ladies would always talk of nature. They were nature. My favorite lesson was one about the trees. I love trees.

There is a mighty oak that grows in my yard. It towers well above our two-story house. It is the tallest tree for miles around. I cannot encircle it with my arms because it has grown for many years. I can sit under the tree and feel its energy in me. On our property three maple trees also stand. Maple trees have a different personality. When I sit near them, they often like to talk to each other. The oak is a more solitary tree in contrast to the maples.

There are no pine trees on our property. Pines are my favorite tree. They hold more wisdom than the other trees. They are the keepers of time. They don't forget who they are as they slumber between seasons. They carry their knowledge through the years.

My ladies helped me to learn from the trees. "Do you see, dear one, how the way the oak grows creates the quality of the wood that is its gift to you? The oak feels stronger than the birch, which is its cousin. The oak acquires this strength by slow, steady growth. The roots of the oak go deeper than the surface trees. It won't succumb to drought as easily, nor will the winds be able to uproot it. It finds a source deep within the earth to nourish itself."

The pines I love carry a scent that always lifts my heart. A pine tree is soft. You can bend its branches. I love to pet its needles. You can slip under the enfolding skirt of a pine and understand more fully what it is like to be a tree. My ladies say the pine gives much to the world. Its wood is softer and easier to work with.

I love it when the ladies come to me. Nature has so much to teach us. Hats off to the ladies. They deserve the respect and consideration that taking off your hat in their presence signifies. Thank you, ladies. Thank you.

There is something about a true lady. Can you feel it?

73

My Record Is Good

Being out in the mornings alone was good for my soul. I can read better when the things around me don't distract me. One of my favorite things to read is the police. Being psychic can have its advantages. I attribute my flawless driving record to the fact that I am psychic. I am one of the guiltiest people in the world when it comes to speeding. I have yet to be caught because I often feel when the police are nearby. The police are so easy to read. They telegraph their thoughts because they think along a singular path. My fear is that I know there is a cop out there who will be daydreaming instead of thinking. He will catch me someday.

More times than I can count have I narrowly avoided getting a ticket because I hear policemen thinking. There is a part of me that feels others feeling and a different part that hears people thinking. Policemen are a good example because their thoughts are so strong as they sit there in their hiding spots, looking for people to turn the wrong way. I was about to make an illegal left turn because I didn't notice the sign that forbade the turn. I was a good four feet into the turn when I heard a thought of joy. *I got one.*

I still couldn't see the police car, but I knew it was there. I completed the most unusual right turn that resembled a fishing hook. I waved to the police officer as I passed the car, which had been unnoticeable from the corner where I started.

Traffic stories are so much fun. I had a strange thought one morning as I woke up to go on my route. I wondered why a car would be following me without its headlights on. That thought quickly left, and I forgot about it.

Hours later, unbeknownst to me, the police were following me as I walked down the street, delivering papers. When I approached my van, the police turned on their lights. Someone had called them about a suspicious person walking around at night. They knew I was OK because they had spent the last half hour following me without their lights on.

Thoughts are things. Feelings are things. I may not be able to physically put my finger on them, but they can touch me in a way that makes me pick them up. I cannot read everyone's thoughts. The easiest thoughts to read are the ones directed at me the way the policeman thought of me as he caught me turning wrong.

The reality of the situation is that thoughts are things. Thoughts are things separate from time because I pick them up in the in-between time of yet to come. In the magic moments between sleep and awareness lies the connection between body and soul, between time and timelessness, between real and yet-to-be real.

That is the reason I can do the things I do. My sensitivity to thoughts makes me able to pick them up out of thin air. Thoughts can travel through time. That is the reason I can pick things up before they happen. All of time exists on the spirit level; that is why I appear to be jumping through time.

There is another example of this. Once again upon waking, I remembered something yet to come. I saw myself wrapping a ribbon around and around a table. *Why would I do such a thing?* was all I was thinking.

Later that day I was at my children's school, helping for a special event. The children had written letters, and they were sending them off airmail attached to balloons. The teacher asked me to cut lengths of ribbon to attach to each balloon. I remembered my dream and cut the ribbons as I had seen myself doing so earlier. Only this time I did it for real.

My life was showing me that feelings and thoughts are real. Time is pliable. This isn't what I am taught on earth. I would have to ask my friends about this.

Understanding why something works helps us to use it more freely. This is doing instead of wondering.

74

The Law

In time my friends were also present during my waking hours. They were amazed at how well we all drove together on earth. They commented on how well everything flowed so smoothly. Most of the time there were no accidents.

I told them we had all agreed on a set of laws that allowed us to drive smoothly. I also pointed out that the law wasn't always followed, and then we did have problems. They still thought it was quite an accomplishment that we could all get along so well. I was more amazed that we got along at all; it was rush hour after all.

My friends entertained me during rush hour with their take on laws. The law would change depending on where you were. If you were in England, you drove on the left side of the road. If you were in Canada, you must drive on the right side of the road. It was the law. There was a reason for this law. There would be consequences if you didn't obey the law.

The law is a thought made solid enough to be real. The reasons for the law are more than the prevention of accidents. The law shows us how to get along. When you focus on the punishment instead of the peace, you never see the purpose. The purpose of the driving law is so traffic flows smoothly. The punishment will be the accident when you go against the flow. The law illustrates how to conduct your life so it will go smoothly.

A law is a basic example of a set of rules used to guide our lives. There have been many laws through time. The rules are a little different depending on where you live, but the effect is the same. There is also a spiritual law that differs depending on where you are.

The Golden Rule we live by has an Eastern cousin known as karma. Buried deep inside these two diverse laws are the same theory. The only difference is what side you drive on. The Golden Rule of "Do unto others as you would have them do unto you" is the same as the biblical law of "As you sow, so shall you reap." The understanding of these laws is also in the Eastern understanding of cause and effect known as karma

Laws are funny things. They can illustrate the problems we have when we separate the material world from the physical one. In the law are two sides, the letter of the law and the spirit of the law. The laws are written for a purpose. When the purpose is no longer being served, the law will change. The laws aren't written so we can punish people. The laws are written so there will be guidelines to peace. The Old Testament has many laws. Moses gave us ten laws. Jesus gave us only one law to live by. The law of love is what he preached. It doesn't matter what side of the road we drive on if we all get along. The purpose of the law is what is important.

My life was becoming a series of "ahaus." It's that moment when a light goes off in your head, and you realize what is happening. It is when you see the coincidences and connections, when all the teachings you have studied come forward into reality. The lesson of spirituality is to be lived and not only learned.

What law or rule did you break to be able to progress?

_____

_____

75

Diving into Meditation

I learned that when you are meditating, you are doing something. You are paying attention. You are waiting. Then it will sneak up on you, and in an instant, you will notice something. You will notice that you are back. You won't notice when you go away, but you will notice that suddenly you are back.

There is a favorite meditation that always works for me. I have found that there isn't a little monkey that toys with me and distracts me. We are taught early on to look for a problem. That sets us up to be negative people. The root of many problems we have in the world comes from the negative thinking. The spirit taught me just to observe, to see it and move on without negative thinking. Meditation works better when you think of it as diving for pearls.

When you dive, you watch your breath. You breathe in and hold it. You breathe out and hold it. You wait. You may notice that you have forgotten to breathe. You were kind of suspended. That was an instant of timelessness in spirit that is called nirvana. A small, small piece of the all.

Now for the pearl part. Take another breath and picture yourself not in a meadow but on a boat, jumping in and diving to the bottom for pearls. Hold your breath as you go. Reach for the pearl and grab it and then resurface. Breathe. Breathe and dive again.

Next time you feel the rhythm of the meditation interrupted by the knowing that you are back, look at your hand and *know* that you returned from the all with just a little pearl of wisdom. Something to hold onto.

With enough practice, you will be able to investigate the pearl and remember. Spirit is timeless. Once you have entered, you can reenter at any time. The pearl will pull you back in. Feel it in your hand. It is like a key.

Our friends (not just mine anymore) give us encouragement as we go.

76

Instructions

Instructions for meditation were never really given. You can be given instructions on how to play basketball. You must really start doing it to learn the game. The same is true for meditation. Starting off slowly with baby steps is expected. You will get better at things, and then you will start to run. It takes practice, but you will get there.

My friends aren't good at rules. That must be why I love them so much. They are more interested in results. My friends always gave illustrations on the magic blackboard in the cove.

They started with the standard chakra map used in the book I worked with to verify what was said. This is the wonderful colored illustration of the chakra system. Ben was standing in front of the class, so small and yet so mighty.

"Today we will work with the system. The most important thing to know is that it is a system. All the parts must work together. Nothing stands alone. Even you, my child, are waking up to your place in a bigger system."

With the long sleeve of his robe, he erased the chakra system on the board in a single swish. In its place was a triangle. *This* is the basis of the system.

More on this later. For now, you can get familiar with the chakras.

PART 7

Next-Generation Teachings

77

Reread

The sections I write are all short. Alton coaches me to say what I want to say and be done with it. The reader will then be free to think about it. The reader will then be free to re-read it because it is so rich with thought. You can also write a note in the space after each section. Writing about the section will help like writing a journal helps you focus your thoughts. In the reread, you might think differently as you have learned more. Comment again as you can now see how you have grown.

When I first started writing many years ago, I didn't want to write just another book about development. I told my teachers, "This is *my* book." It is about me. It is about the closet. Now that I am older and I hope wiser, I think the rest of the book will be about *you*.

Your thoughts?

_____

_____

78

Prerequisites

As in all forms of learning, you first need the basics. You learn the alphabet and the small words before you can use all the letters to be able to write what you want to express. This will take years. Small steps along the way of your path. There are twenty-six letters in the alphabet. There are at least that many steps in spiritual development. Most are learned without even noticing you are learning. At this point, you are experiencing things and learning on the streets.

Contemplation is a good example. You think about things. It just comes naturally. Wondering about things is another good example. Wondering is a good way to attract things to you that you want to learn about. Listening and noticing things are needed too. I had to go to remedial discipline class with Ben. Discipline keeps you on the path. There is more; there is always more.

Mediumship is one of the prerequisites. Going to mediums is a good hook. When you go to mediums, they will pique your interest in the unseen other side. The motivation may be to hear from your loved ones, but the effect is to start you having interest in the other side.

Readings are another great hook. When you are young, you are read to by someone who already knows what all the strange symbols are. The letters have no meaning to you yet. Those strange letters and symbols you have yet to understand. Your interest is piqued. You start to learn the language of the spirits. The spirits don't own nouns. Nouns to them are symbols of meaning, like the basketball under the shirt of a woman means she is pregnant. Some, like dreams, are a common language. Others, like the basketball, are a personal language.

Healing can interest many. Understanding why you have an

issue and then how to correct it is a wonderful talent. Forgiveness is a common roadblock to spiritual health. This will need to be addressed later in this book. Forgiveness is hard because it is part of the next-generation (or next-gen) teachings. You will get there.

Cards and the stars can be a good start. There are many cards. Horoscopes have twelve categories to learn about. Twelve ways of being. Twelve qualities that can be possessed. Why do we not have twelve chakras? We do. Those are also part of the next-gen teachings.

What got you hooked and started on your path?

_____

_____

Shade or Shadow

My husband and I loved to travel. We often flew to new destinations. It was on one of these trips that I realized something. I was looking out the window as we took off. I marveled at the shadow of a tree. I wondered why I always saw it as shade and never thought about how it would look like from above. Which view is the correct view? Both views have validity. Both are true. The difference is where you are looking from. Do you look at spirituality from the EGO (Earth Guide Only), or do you look from a higher understanding.

Decisions will have to be made. Will you be like Columbus and try to bring the European life to the new world? Will you get to know the natives like Marco Polo did?

Decide if you will look for more and progress. You can also decide not to work on development and digress. Development is *work*. To start, all you need to do is decide.

Decide if you will listen to your guides like King Arthur listened to Merlin. Your teacher doesn't need to be unseen. Your teacher can be part of the material world.

Decide if you want intuition or inspiration. Intuition is great to have. It got you this far. Now you can strive to get inspiration. Inspiration is from the spirit.

Decide if you want to keep going with the crowd. You can also decide to go within and look for the spirit inside you. Development is a singular path. Development isn't found inside a group. Your path is no longer a freeway; it is a singular path. Along the path you will find counselors and teachers. Along the path you will find what has been missing. The missing link. / The father. \ The son. _ The holy spirit. /\ The missing link is the holy spirit.

Will you think and then decide?

Numbers

I can start with an easy lesson. The lesson of numbers, not numerology. After living with my teachers for some time, I realized that many of their lessons were about the journey, the progression, like the earlier lesson on the garden when you learned to look around you more. Numbers are like that too. This section looks at the physical shape of the numbers.

1. You are straight and tall.
2. You are confused. Have you ever seen such an awkward number?
3. You start to straighten yourself out. You will develop with the spirit and material. You aren't yet complete.
4. You want to concentrate on the spirit because it is so wonderful. You are likely to tip over because you aren't yet balanced.
5. You are at another awkward time in your life. You aren't sure which direction to go.
6. You decide to ground yourself. You are living in this world after all.
7. You still hear the call of the spirit.
8. You understand now that you are both. You are balanced, living both.
9. You can now use the spirit more than just the material side of yourself.
10. You realize you are both. Both will become one number working alongside each other.

Development by the numbers. You can count on it.

81

Chakras

I may as well just start now with a biggie. I hope you are wearing steel-toed boots, because this is the stepping-on-people's-toes part. The map my teachers use for the chakras is different. The magic board behind the teacher illustrates what the lesson is. This lesson started with a triangle. The first three chakras create the triangle. The / of the triangle is the first chakra. The next chakra is the energy of the unit, and then is the \, the finishing touch. It is said the gut is the lower brain, the part that can figure out what this life is all about. This is the home of the gut feelings that guide you in early life.

Let us start the next set. There is a higher chakra that is calling. The heart opens you to grow with love of others. This is the first time you exit the simple, singular self. This is where you notice others around you. /The throat chakra means you begin to speak to them. \Your yin assertion gets to work. The yang gets to work by bringing in what it sees and observes. /\ together. _The higher brain is completing the triangle as it pieces everything together.

Now is the part of the lesson that exits the standard understanding of the chakras. Because of your meditations over the years, you have opened the eighth chakra. For the sake of this book, I found it, so I can name it. It is the unity chakra. There is more on how this happens when we get to the meditation section. For now, all you need to know is that you have just left linear time and thinking. You have entered the spirit part of you. The next triangle is starting.

Things are different now. This triangle will be pointing down. The next three sides of the triangle are the double-named chakras. Is it the root or the base? Is it the sacral or the navel? Is it the brow or the third eye? I won't tell you. The study of this is for you to anchor them in place.

Next, yes, there is a next. There is the calling of the twelfth chakra. This one really blew my mind. The triangles multiplied until the chakra was like a starburst and then a lotus blossom. All for now.

It does seem overwhelming. Just work piece by piece. Work it out and write it out.

82

Hearing the Call

The hearing of the call comes naturally. The calling of the heart opens you up and allows you to exit the thinking of only yourself. Not everyone will answer the call. Not answering illustrates how you will digress as spoken about earlier. You become narcissistic. This is where deciding comes in. Progress or digress—the choice isn't an easy one. The decision could go either way. The choice is made in the early years of a life. The older you are, the more likely you are to still focus on only self. This is a very pivotal moment in any life. Decide!

Answering the call of the heart will allow you to love. Like earlier in the book during my NDE, I wondered what could possibly be better. Then there is another calling, the unity chakra. You don't know about a person until you walk a mile in his or her shoes. The unity chakra allows you to walk in the shoes of another so you can learn. The unity chakra allows you to forgive because you walk a mile in his or her shoes. The unity chakra allows you to be a medium. The unity chakra allows you to do readings.

I know you have answered the call of love. Will you answer the next call?

83

The Call of Unity

During my NDE when I reached love, I didn't know what could possibly be better. I wanted to stay there because love was so good and comforting. I would have stayed there had I not heard the call. Looking around you more, you will notice strange things. Coincidences and synchronicities will pepper your life. Wondering about why this is happening, you might answer the call and investigate it, or you might decide not to progress and stay where you are. Will you digress? How can love possibly be a digression? Everything has a shelf life, even love. There is more; there is always more.

Now you are at number seven. You reached out for more in the spirit, and you have found love. This is a very dangerous stage. Love is great but loving only makes you unbalanced. The number seven is the most likely number to fall over and crash. You need the balance of eight.

Will you answer the call of unity? This is a hard decision. Write about deciding now.

_____

_____

84

Empaths

Empaths have answered the call of the eighth chakra. Or rather, the eighth chakra is universally open to any on the path, like it or not. The critical mass has been reached, and as a member of all, the unity chakra opened. This has led to the unity chakra being open when the earlier chakras have yet to be understood. The answer to this problem is to work on the earlier chakras.

When I was young, crystals were all the rage. Everyone was working with them. I instead needed to be grounded. I instead became interested in rocks. The talent of unity helped me to be able to read rocks. Holding the different kinds of rocks gave me a picture of how it had been created. Better than that, it grounded me. I was no longer an open target for unity. I could control it.

Missing steps along the way makes missing pieces. Claim the missing now. Will you write about your grounding?

_____

_____

85

Yin and Yang and One

Yin and yang are a good example of what is missing. The yin and yang symbol holds so much. There are two sides, and even a little bit of each side is held in the other. We are so used to thinking in duality that we don't even know we are limiting ourselves. That little piece of the other side is unity starting. Hearing the call will break you out of duality and start the concept of multiplicity.

The missing piece is now noticing that the two sides are encased in the circle. They are encased within the complete circle. There are the putting it all together and digesting and making sense of what you have acquired as you reach out and bring it in. The breath is like this too. You breathe in, and then you breathe out. Do you notice what is missing? The part where you use and absorb the oxygen and process it so you can exhale what is good for the plants. This makes you part of the "all."

With that in mind, there is a difference between *all* and *becoming one*. You and others can see the difference. When you use the eighth chakra, you think you are joining all others. You are not. You are becoming one with others. The all? The all is much more. That is the twelfth, which blows your mind. There is more; there is always more.

Number one is the beginning. There is more. Becoming one with others is the first step in merging with the all.

86

Meditate, Contemplate, and All

What is the missing piece again? For many, there are two missing pieces. Most people meditate. Many people forget to contemplate. Thinking about something helps you to change your direction. Your spin on any matter will create your view of the world. Confucius would always come up with a different way of thinking about something. Hearing him, you can see he is right. Contemplate and turn things around in your mind to see something from many angles. This allows you to progress instead of going along with the crowd.

My friends had me look at a statue. It was a woman walking. I then had to walk around the woman and see her from a different view. It wasn't the woman I noticed anymore. It was the folds in her dress that showed she was in a hurry. The stiff statue could still portray the movement of the dress. From behind, I saw more. The back of a leg was showing, and the sandals she was wearing became evident. Walking further, I noticed she was carrying a basket. Going back to where I had started, I then saw a peaceful look on her face. When I looked more, I saw more.

Contemplate what you are studying. Look at it from different angles. Imagine that it had a past. Wonder about what happens in the future. Work on seeing it as another would see it. Then you can take the next step. The missing piece now is figuring it out. Digesting it. Using it. Did thinking about something make you change your ideas? Did thinking about it make you change your direction? Meditation is a three-step process too. Meditate, contemplate, figure it out, and grow.

There is another example of the missing piece. There is the Old

Testament. Then the next step is the New Testament. Then the part where things are put together and learned. The living testament. That is why you must live the lessons. You then totally understand the lessons, and you can own them.

What do you think? Contemplation is deeper thinking.

87

Channeling

I admit that I do channel mostly while I am writing and sometimes while I am talking. When I write, I am coached. This isn't automatic writing. This is *my* story, not theirs. When I channel and they are talking, I don't disappear as Edgar Casey did. I insisted early on to sit and view as they speak. I also want to hear what they have to say. This is the next generation thinking. Things don't have to be like they always were. Break that mold. I am coming out of the closet with this now because I feel the time is short. As recently as this year, I experienced a put-down for channeling. The closet is still somewhat my safe place.

It took years to start to channel. Being one is a lengthy step.

88

One More Confession

Here is one more confession before I go on. I am very narrow minded. I am open to new things and ways, but there is only so much I can do. I had to learn to focus on just one thing. In the story of this life, I also suffered a brain injury from a rollover accident. This caused me to need to make my life small and narrow so I could cope. In researching for this book, I wanted to observe a good medium. Somehow there came the opportunity to get to know one. I am amazed at the diversity of his knowledge. I am respectful of how he trained and worked to gain the talents he has. I truly admire him for his giving ways. He also, it seems, is in the last act. He is teaching as he works now. The last thing I want to say is "Thank you."

Whom can you learn from? Not just in school but in the game of life?

89

Karma

Put on your steel-toed boots again ("your shit-kicking boots," like my brother would say). Karma isn't what you think. We are taking it entirely too personally. Karma is cause and effect. Karma doesn't extend to other lives we think we will live. There is no record keeper who makes sure you are repaid for the good and punished for the bad. When I was young and in my poetry phase, I wrote a piece to my boyfriend. "You aren't it; you are just the one who got hit." We had a fight because I was upset about something else. That was the cause. The effect was that I treated him badly. This is something to contemplate. What you do will have a ripple effect on others. You will also walk into the ripples of others. Some of the ripples will be like a tsunami like my poor boyfriend was. Some will be so small that they simply have no effect. It is not all about you. You are only a piece of what is around you.

Living in the now is how Karma is. It is not about deserving. It is about just living.

90

Life Goes On

The first half of the book ended with "The Continuation of Life." With all due respect to my friends—and there is much respect to be given—there is more. Their writing is almost lyrical. It's hard to digest what is in the story. My writing is an example of applying the teachings. Absorbing a new thought is like absorbing a new word.

You look up the definition. Then you apply it in a sentence. Now you are really the master of the new word.

You are now on your way to becoming a master.

91

Past Lives

I hope you still have your steel-toed boots on. This is even stepping on my toes. I believed the lives I was remembering were *my* past lives. The strongest one for me was the life where the person I thought I was had her throat slit. I have had throat problems most of my life. When I was a child, I had tonsillitis so often that they could no longer wait for it to go down because the tonsils never went down. The doctors took my tonsils anyway. This led to my first NDE. I understand how lives gone by can affect current life.

When I became an adult, I saw the scenario of the life gone by. I saw the woman and her friend leaving a pub in old England. Two men attacked them and slit their throats. I saw the woman touch her bleeding throat as the hot blood brought steam to the scene. The dying thoughts of the lady were, *I should never have picked up the mug.*

I once was on your side with the past lives being *my* past lives. The belief was like sitting in the shade of a tree only to also see later that it was seen as a shadow from above. The lives you are remembering aren't *your* lives. It was once thought that we were the center of everything. The sun and moon and stars went around us. Then we learned we were part of something bigger. We are a small piece of something bigger than we could ever imagine. The lives aren't all about us.

When I had my NDE, there was the part where I could see how I affected others. I could feel how the other person felt as I dealt him or her undeserved karma. Others who had accounts of an NDE noticed this, and the process inspired them to change. (It didn't intuit them to change; it inspired them to change. It is now about the spirit.) The merging with another is more than just a merge. The merging is becoming one with others. You are now a small part of the one. Now that you are part of the one, you have access to others who are there in the one. The knowing of others is the effect of the eighth chakra opening.

Look around you more. See more?

92

Preparing for a New Life

I can now remember planning the life I am living now. When we pass to the other side, there is the merging with others. This event goes deeper. Your life is becoming one with others. As a member of the all, you have access to all past lives.

In the spirit, we can see the events of earth. We can see more, but for the purpose of this book, we will look at earth. My higher self can see what is happening on earth and what is going on soon. My interests lie in wondering how I can help with the development of those on earth. I picked two categories: spiritual gifts and the curse of alcoholism.

Planning a new life is sort of like packing for a vacation. You are about to visit a place for a short amount of time. You first must decide where to go. I didn't want to lose being the spirit, so I chose a setting where I could believe in the gifts of the spirit. That was a setting of Catholics who believe in saints. In the same setting was the problem of alcoholism. Now that I knew where I was going, I had to pack my bags.

I had to pack for a life that had addiction in it. I chose a life that knew not to drink. I also wanted a life that retained the talents of spiritual abilities. I chose the life of a person who practiced knowing. I don't know how else to describe this man. He was in very old times. He just knew things. His spirit stayed in contact with his higher self. He knew. I finished packing the essentials, many basic talents I would need for the trip, many lives of value to emulate. I had been on many trips before. I knew what to pack.

There was one more facet to the jewel of this life I needed. I wanted to be able to express and share the gifts of spirituality. I didn't want to just do "it." I wanted to show how "it" works. There was a life in which she was killed for the things she could do. Her dying thoughts were, *If people knew more about the gift, they wouldn't be afraid of it.*

Planning a life is like planning a vacation. You don't usually travel alone. There are others who plan to go with you. They are busy packing their bags to go with what they are planning. My daughter planned a short life. She knew the setting of the life we were going to would make her susceptible to a brain chemistry imbalance. She knew I needed to learn about this to understand my addiction to alcohol. She also packed a life full of love. It was as a mother in that life, who dearly loved her child.

My husband planned a life that intersected with my life in only one aspect. He chose a life in which he knew he had to protect me. He had other things to work on. My son is not at all interested in the spirit. His interests lie in knowing a thing, not knowing about the spirit but knowing about science. To each his or her own.

What did you pack for the life you are in? What qualities did you need for the trip?

93

Opening a Crack to Start

The NDE opened the eighth chakra for me. The opening of the eighth chakra explains how a medium and reader can operate. I know a good medium who said it took two years of meditation to really get started. Meditation is the way to open the eighth chakra. We all already own the eighth chakra. That is why you can know things about a loved one who is in trouble. The energy of love can open a crack in the eighth. You are connected. I suspect many have experienced this event. Now is the question of why the eighth opens with meditation.

Did you ever open a crack and just know?

PART 8

Meditation

94

Meditation

It isn't common to have a heading for each short section. We do this to bring attention to the separate parts of meditation. We do this so that during the reread you can look it up easily as a reference method. This isn't a read-it-once-and-be-done-with-it book. This is a read-it-again-and-again-so-you-can-pick-up-any-missing-pieces book.

Are you ready for the biggie? Meditation is like going to the gym. There are different machines for the different things you are working on. That is why meditation is so important. There are many aspects to meditation. Before we start on the practice of meditation, we can first find it in our everyday lives. Daydreaming is much like meditation. You kind of zone out and suddenly snap back in. Runners also do a meditation cousin. You go and go, and suddenly, you are gone. Occupying your mind with a simple task can get you to the goal. You can color or knit, and then suddenly you kind of leave yourself behind.

You were meditating and didn't know it. Did you feel better after you returned each time?

_____

_____

95

Be Still

Now you will need another skill to proceed. When I was sent to detention with Ben, being still was the first thing he taught. Ben said to sit. That is all he said. I sat. I dared not do anything else. So being still is turning off everything around you. The next two days were just sitting. I find it is easiest for me to just wait. If you are attentive, the mind doesn't wander. If wandering starts, just breathe deeply and wait again. You can usually enter the stillness within three deep breaths. That is my method. I know others are on a different path.

We are so used to doing. Being still is about just being.

96

Breath

Step two is taking the breath that opens the eighth chakra. I find it's best to concentrate on breathing in for a count of four. You can then hold your breath for a count of four. Holding your breath is once again the missing piece, the step where you utilize the oxygen.

You can then slowly exhale for a count of four. I also know each will have his or her own path and use different methods.

Ben taught about the breath. He said to follow his breath. I learned to breathe, to think about breathing, to *be* the breath. The next five days were about breathing. Ben then asked whether I had any questions. Of course, I did. I asked why breath was so important.

The magic whiteboard was then behind him. The board then illustrated the known seven chakras. The board turned the model around so we could see the back. The eighth is the first chakra to be at the back. Have you noticed that when you first start feeling spirit, it is from behind? The feelings then proceed to your sides and later to the front so you can see better. Spirit is then enveloping you because you are one.

Just breathe and write.

97

The Gland for the New Chakra

Each chakra is activated by a gland. This is also true for the eighth. The gland is the carotid gland, which is located at the back and base of the brain. This gland isn't understood, and little information can be found about it. This gland is affected by the amount of oxygen in the carotid artery. The controlled breathing regulates the amount of oxygen in the blood. Long-time mediators, upon autopsy, have a larger carotid gland.

Just breathe.

98

Guided Meditation

Many people do guided meditation. Guided meditation is when you listen to a person or recording that takes you on a visual trip. You are then guided into the world of spirit. This is an important component of meditation. You are learning that you can create a picture of what you desire. The most common is walking along a path and meeting with a guide or loved one. You may not realize it, but you are talking to your higher self and stating what you are looking for. The communication has started.

Whom did you visit? Whom will you visit now that you know more?

99

Long-Time Meditating

You don't need to spend a long time each day in meditation. You do need to meditate regularly, however. It is like when you are walking through a deep forest. The path at first is hard as you encounter obstacles and branches. Each time you walk the path, the going gets easier. You are laying down a foundation. The path then will get easier. Meditation takes concentration. Meditation needs a regime, the same time each day in total dedication. Find a place and time where there will be no distractions or interruptions. Meditation needs to have no interruptions. Meditation is serious business.

There came a time when I developed a new talent. You too can do it. In the old *Get Smart* TV show, there was a cone of silence that came down to keep others out. I found that when I was working or meditation, the cone came down in a crowded room. I didn't really develop it; it just happened. It can happen for you too. Try it.

Remedial discipline helped me to do this. Do you need help too?

_____

_____

100

Getting There

It's like that old joke. "How do I get to the Broadway?" Practice, dear, practice. You must work on your craft to get there. The same is true with meditation. You will get there. It will take practice. More than practice—it will take work and time.

It does take time, but each step has a payoff. Keep up the good work.

101

Enjoy Meditating

Imagine a place where you will be free from interruptions, a quiet, peaceful place with no overthinking issues. Meditation takes concentration. Meditation needs a regime, the same time each day in total dedication. This is called "me time." You deserve it. You need it

What you enjoy you will do more. You will look forward to meditating.

102

Being One

I hope your boots are the tall kind. I'm about to destroy what you think spirit is. It's not "a" spirit. Spirit is no longer a noun. Spirit is an energy. Spirit is the feeling of oneness, joining with others. Spirit is felt when you are at a sporting event. Everyone is joined in the fun. The eighth isn't a part of the physical world. The eighth is at the back so you know you are exiting the physical. Yourself, your soul, is a tiny piece of the spirit, like at a large stadium when you see a football game. You join and become one. You don't disappear. You are still there.

Many people wonder how a loved one can still be there or even be anywhere after he or she has passed away. In an NDE you experience the feeling of knowing how another felt. This is deeper; you are merging and becoming one. You are always there. You are just a part of something bigger just like at the football game.

You will be surprised by some of the changes in spirit. Pleasantly surprised.

103

Many Paths

When I work with Alton, I can meditate for about a half hour. After that much time, I need a break. I go to the living room to watch TV and play solitaire on the phone. I relax. As I start to relax more, Alton will slip in little hints on the next section. This is a good illustration of a different path. Being still is very much like relaxing. You can sew, knit, color, go for a run, or do many other things that clear the deck of your mind. Spirit then can slip in things to you. How often do you think of something out of the blue that has nothing to do with your normal day? You think of a person you haven't seen in a long time. You see her the next day. You think of a loved one, and suddenly you want to call her. There are many paths to spirit.

You have learned to work with spirit. Spirit will learn to work with you.

104

Exiting Ego

There are many paths. There is also a big intersection for becoming one. Just being a member of the human race can open things up for you. Becoming one is a natural process. Your eighth chakra doesn't need to be opened to meet your guides. You already own all the chakras. They already work for you. You just need to be open and ask. Becoming one with my husband was a very comfortable thing. Becoming one with my teachers was a very comfortable thing.

This process is known as "exiting ego," this leaving the simple self behind and becoming part of a group. Exiting ego is needed to start to *be* spirit. Then you can see that karma isn't all about you. Then you can see that reincarnation is just incarnation. There is nothing personal about past lives. Taking nothing personally also makes you less judgmental. When you are less judgmental, you have less to forgive. Forgiveness is the last biggie. We will get to that. Your personal ego becomes less and less important as you join others.

Are your views changing? Are you changing for the better?

_____

_____

105

As Above So Below

Most of us are born and bred Westerners. Ben was very important in giving me the missing pieces of the East. We have the chakra sets of three, with each leading to a higher set. What you learned in first grade is still true in later years. The same idea is true for so many things as we progress. The concept of the micro (small) pieces is true for the macro (bigger) pieces. I told you there are at least twenty-six different things to know as we progress.

Most of the things to learn you already know. You just have to learn to use them.

106

Narcissists

I know I went on and on about answering the call of love. Perhaps the best way to show how important it is may be to show when progress is lacking. As above so below. Narcissists can spoil those they are around. The singular thinking also spoils the one who is a narcissist. As above, the country now in the news is a country full of those who think only about themselves. Corruption is all about thinking only of themselves or their tribe. The comfort zone is only with people like themselves. That kind of thinking can make neighbors not get along. That kind of thinking made the North and South go to war. That kind of thinking makes the Catholics and Protestants of England fight. That kind of thinking makes wars. If you cannot be a good example, be a horrible reminder.

Can you see how important it is to make the right decisions?

107

Stagnation

Not answering the call of unity will have consequences. We all know that stagnant water will begin to smell. The stagnant water is no longer serving a purpose.

I am part of the hippie generation. I know that if you aren't part of the solution, you are part of the problem. You become a problem if you don't move on. You become like Christopher Columbus; stuck in the ways you are used to. You destroy others, like the Indians, instead of understanding others. There is no unity.

Can you see how important it is to take the next step?

108

Prayer and Meditation

Prayer is talking to God. Meditation is listening to God. You are now learning the two-way street of communication. Prayer in communication isn't the same old route of repeating the holy words. That also has its place. Prayer now is reaching out to God or all. You can now get comfortable sitting in the presence of the all while in meditation, focusing your thoughts. No longer do monkeys distract you. Focusing your thoughts brings you closer to the all.

It is a two-way street. Unity is all about that. Whom did you unite with?

109

Forgiveness

Meditation was the biggie. Forgiveness is the hardest. Many cannot or won't do it. Forgiving becomes easier with the next set of chakras. The eighth called you. You got comfortable with becoming more by learning unity. The three unity chakras got you ready for the next step. Now the twelfth is calling you. The twelfth is the place for many gifts. Understanding is one. There is also the suddenly great feeling of "Wow, now I get it." Epiphanies are those things that are greater than love. You got there because you sought more. There is more; there is always more. You have at times used the gifts of the twelfth. You have always owned all the chakras.

You will find forgiveness easier now. Who needs to forgive? Who needs to be forgiven?

_____

_____

110

Forgiving My Mother

I never even knew I had to forgive my mother. I was holding a grudge against her. I knew I would never be like her. She was distant and uncaring. I didn't realize at the time that I was nursing a wound. When I had my own children, I made sure the children knew I cared about them. I was involved in their lives. My mother never once came to any of my basketball games. I made sure I was at all the events of school and sports for them. I thought I was raising my kids better. I still think I am. I didn't realize that I was healing myself.

At the time I didn't realize I was judging her. I just knew I was hurt. Becoming one with her brought me to an understanding and freed me to finally love her. I learned that forgiveness comes from understanding the other person. "To each their own" has deeper meaning when it comes to forgiveness. I found it was a generational thing. In her generation, the woman stayed home, cared for the house, and raised the children. My mother had six children. She was overwhelmed. It was all she could do to hold things together. I walked a mile in her shoes and understood better. I even came to admire her for all she did. Forgiveness came because I understood things better.

Look deep into another person. Walk that mile in his or her shoes. Then forgiveness will happen.

111

Forgiving My Father

I knew I had to forgive my father. I knew he was a bad man and an alcoholic. When I learned to understand things better, I learned he was bad mostly when he was drunk. He was drunk quite often. How did I learn to understand and forgive him? I will thank my children. My children inherited my blonde hair, blue eyes, and a brain chemistry problem. My father and brothers were self-medicating with alcohol.

This root problem caused many other problems. Back then there were no answers for mental health. I am eternally grateful for the attention being paid to mental health now. No more wasted lives.

I saw how difficult life is when you have a brain chemistry problem. My children also came to have problems as they entered their late teens. Suddenly, it was like part of them left, and another part came in. They had such problems. Then as they went on medication, they returned.

Understanding the root of the problem brought forgiveness. More than that, it brought a solution to the root problem.

112

Forgiving My Husband

Many times, you marry the type of person you are comfortable with. I married someone who had drug problems. The story was told earlier in this book. He did get clean. I hadn't yet forgiven him for all the years and all the harm. He was in NA for years. It took years to get things together again. I experienced the same years as I slowly learned to trust him again. Forgiveness isn't an instant thing. It isn't like when you go into a confessional and the priest forgives all your sins.

My husband didn't have a brain chemistry problem. He had an upbringing problem. I lived in a dysfunctional family. My husband's family was abusive. Drugs were his coping mechanism. The lying that came along with drug use was a big factor in his upbringing. Lying was a way to control those around them as a way of life. Beatings and put-downs were another method of control.

Forgiving my husband came in time. My in-laws also treated me terribly. Loving my husband gave me more people to forgive. It took years, but I finally figured it out. I didn't need to forgive them. They were none of my business. It was enough that my family stayed together. We all grew together. Maybe the lesson is to just stay away from toxic people. NA taught me something too. Accept what I cannot change. Have courage to change what I can and wisdom to know the difference.

Sometimes forgiveness takes time. As you grow, you can forgive more. Sometimes you don't even need to forgive. You just need to let go.

113

Forgiving My In-Laws

A few weeks before my husband died, he told me something that changed everything. Learning a life lesson doesn't come only from a guide. Learning also comes from those you live with. Yet another lie was revealed. Very early in our marriage, my mother-in-law told a big lie about me. Everyone believed her. It was what they were used to. This lie damaged the relationship with my in-laws. I became the outlaw.

My husband loved me and the children. He stood by me. The distance between him and his family helped him to be able to heal the harm that had been done to him. I am so grateful for the new man he worked so hard to become. When we found out about the big lie a few weeks before his passing, everything exploded. During a yelling session on the phone, this lie was revealed. I had had enough. I broke all ties with the toxic ways. I would have nothing to do with them anymore. I finally had the wisdom to know the difference.

My husband intervened and talked to his family about the lies. I realized this was his fight and not mine. This was his healing. I didn't need to heal him. He did this all by himself. The closure was a good thing for all involved.

What was it that was said that changed everything? He told me I was a good person, but I have 10 percent that goes bad when I am mad. He said I had helped him. He said I had helped the kids. He said he thought I could help his sister. Hmm. Ten percent. I thought about that. I did love his family, but the percentage that was bad made forgiveness difficult. I could then forgive the whole person because I knew he or she wasn't all bad. I had learned.

Look for the good in the person. Then you can forgive the bad.

114

Forgiving the Assailant

My going to school in the sky started because I had wanted to hurt the person who hurt my daughter. I was taught to heal and not hurt. I was instructed to improve myself by no longer being codependent. I had to work on me. I had to become a better person. School was wonderful. I learned so much. Would I ever have left the closet and gone to school if the assault never happened? Probably not. I guess I made lemonade out of lemons.

That is my side of the event. Even in school I still wanted to find the man and hurt him. At the end of the book, I included a piece I wrote for a class on writing. The writing showed that I can work on me, not on doing something to someone else. I already confessed that I am narrow minded. I prefer to look at it as focused. Focusing is looking at myself and changing myself.

Focusing on the assailant did me no good. Focusing on myself had a big payoff. Eventually, I no longer hated the man as much. I let it go. This is about as close to forgiveness as I guess it can get. The assailant no longer mattered. Living well is the best revenge. Living well is the best solution, both for the man and for my in-laws.

Focusing on the solution and not on the problem gets you to forgiveness.

_____

_____

115

Giving Forgiveness

Forgiving may be hard until you have moved up the chakras. We were stuck in the world of dualities instead of multiplicities. Knowing there is more is now freeing you to think in terms of possibilities. We were taught that things are either right or wrong. This is clear-cut, simple thinking. Understanding motives and thinking about others make you think about more. Is the thief wrong, or is he starving? There is more. Can you give forgiveness when you understand the situation?

Gifting something to someone is a good quality. Can you gift forgiveness?

_____

_____

116

The Twelfth Chakra Is Calling

I really don't know whether the eighth's chakra set, or the calling of the twelfth helped me learn about forgiveness. I think at this point that both were influencing me. The twelfth chakra is very much serendipity

like the last step in my NDE. I knew everything. I understood everything. The things I fought against had a part and a lesson. So did the wicked man who assaulted my daughter. The school healed both me and my daughter.

After my daughter was killed, my husband and I went on a vacation out west. We were at the Grand Canyon when I had a sudden understanding. The canyon is so large that it is in seven different states. I imagined my daughter and I were like little pieces of sand somewhere in the canyon. Somehow, even the big things I worried about came to mean so little. I would come to look more at the bigger picture like in my writing assignment.

Looking around you more will expand yourself. You will become a bigger, better person.

117

"Getting It"

Suddenly, "getting it" is a great feeling. Getting it is the effect of the twelfth chakra. Getting it is the smallest sample of the next step. This is when you grasp what has been taught. The settled feeling is a sign that you got it.

Have you ever gotten an understanding after thinking about it for a while?

_____

_____

118

Understanding

A greater understanding is like graduating to the next grade. You have finished all the prerequisites and are ready to put what you have learned into practice. You have another tool to use in the work you do.

Have you ever thought, I just don't understand? *Think about that.*

_____

_____

119

Epiphanies

The biggest dose of the last chakra is an epiphany. You get such a jolt of everything. I have been touched by this only a few times. Maybe the three sides are these three qualities.

I'm not sure. The starburst is truly a mind-blowing event.

The star has many points, angles, and triangles. I cannot understand it all.

There. I think I am done. No, wait. There is more. There is always more.

The All

There is always more. One more thing. If I cannot be a good example, I will be a horrible reminder. When a person doesn't move on, there is a problem. If you don't progress, you will digress. If a person doesn't answer the call of the love chakra, then that person may become a narcissist. Many here can see the harm that can cause. If you don't answer the call of the unity chakra, that person too becomes a problem. The free love of the sixties illustrates one problem. Further, if we don't learn about others via unity, we are condemned to the noise of hatred of others. Many here can see the problem with this.

All for now. There is more; there is always more.

120

Love Wasn't Enough

It was a time long ago, if fifteen years can be considered long ago, when I hit what I thought was the lowest point in my life. I had to deal with a pain I thought would never go away. Someone had assaulted my young daughter. I was filled with such anger and hatred. I lived every day thinking of ways to get the assailant. I lived every day reliving the events of that day and the days afterward when meetings with police, doctors, and social workers still couldn't bring resolution to the situation. This was a self-perpetuating hell.

I didn't know how to help my daughter, but I knew I had to stay angry, or I wouldn't have the strength to carry on. Anger was literally feeding me, giving me a reason to get up each day. I had to get up so I could be angry again. It was all I knew.

When I lived in this world of hatred, I could see into other worlds, where people were acting out of love. I couldn't understand how anyone could return injury with love. I was certain those loving people could never have had to face the things I had to face. My world was filled with hurt. I was sure the cure for hurt was hatred.

I'm not proud of the way I acted then. I acted the only way I knew how. I was young and had lessons to learn. Slowly the lesson of learning to love found its way into my heart. I had to learn a new way to live, because living in hatred was breaking me.

In this world of hatred was a little corner of love. I still loved my little girl, and she still loved me. Slowly that little bit of love overwhelmed the anger and hatred that were feeding me. Each morning when I got up, I chose to love. Day by day things got better. Eventually, I felt more at home in the world of love than in the world of hatred.

The rewards of learning to live with love weren't fully appreciated until I hit a lower low in my life. I had to bury that same daughter.

I'm so grateful for learning to live in love and escaping the world of anger and hatred. The years between the two lows were filled with love and laughter. She grew to be a wonderful, loving adult. Had we not decided to love, I hate to think of what she would have become.

This new low in my life is teaching me a few things. I sit here and live in the world of loving her. I wake up each day and relive the wonderful days we had together. I recognize this as the same feelings I had fifteen years ago. If I keep living in the world of love, surely I will break. Love isn't enough. I must find a new way to live.

I look out at the world again to see how others could possibly live through something like this. What is the cure for losing someone you love? Thousands were cast into this world on a single day in New York. How do they go on? How do I go on? How do we all go on?

There is a little light I see shining in a corner. Just as I once lived in a world of hatred and saw a world of love, I now look outward and forward and see a world of wisdom and understanding. Each day I get up and choose to see things differently by seeing her life and my life in the larger picture.

If the past can teach me anything, it is that someday I will be grateful I learned to live in wisdom. I'm not there yet. I still cry for the love I lost, but a part of me is learning.

P.S. Years have passed since I wrote this piece. I am now grateful.

Printed in the United States
by Baker & Taylor Publisher Services